21 DAYS

of

DEEPER

PRAYER

*Discover an Extraordinary
Life in God*

JIM MAXIM

with Daniel Henderson

WHITAKER
HOUSE

Boldface type in Scripture quotations indicates the authors' emphasis.

21 Days of Deeper Prayer
Discover an Extraordinary Life in God

www.acts413.net/deeperprayer
www.strategicrenewal.com/21days-deeper-prayer

ISBN: 978-1-64123-634-8
eBook ISBN: 978-1-64123-635-5
Printed in the United States of America
© 2020 by Jim Maxim

Whitaker House
1030 Hunt Valley Circle
New Kensington, PA 15068
www.whitakerhouse.com

Library of Congress Control Number: 2020947405

1 2 3 4 5 6 7 8 9 10 11 〰 27 26 25 24 23 22 21 20

DEDICATION

This book is lovingly dedicated to my grandchildren
Lucy, James, and Dylan Maxim.

Contents

Introduction: Rivers of Living Water..7

Join the Interactive *21 Days of Deeper Prayer* Experience! 13

   1. The Foundation of Prayer... 14

   2. As It Is in Heaven 20

   3. Life as He Intended 25

   4. Holy Spirit, You Are Welcome................................29

   5. Prayer: An Infusion of God's Tailor-Made Grace 33

   6. Prayer Worthy of Our Creator 38

   7. One Extraordinary Day 43

   8. Let's Go to the Other Side...47

   9. What's Waiting There?..51

  10. What About You, Storm Chaser?................................55

  11. Wisdom Will Come into Your Heart 60

  12. Don't Feel Like Praying?..64

  13. Seeking God When Life Is Uncertain......................70

  14. How the Holy Spirit Ignites Our Prayers.................74

  15. Learn to Wrestle Well...80

16. From Darkness to Light...85

17. Snatching Them Out of the Fire................................89

18. Perfect Peace...94

19. Are You Really Praying in Jesus's Name?..................100

20. There Was a Believer...105

21. Moving the Hand that Moves the World.................108

About the Authors..112

Introduction:
Rivers of Living Water

He who believes in Me, as the Scripture said, 'From his innermost being will flow rivers of living water.'"
—John 7:38 (NASB)

I'm so excited you are here with us on this twenty-one-day prayer journey to grow deeper in God. Our prayer for you during this time is exactly this:

> *That the God of our Lord Jesus Christ, the Father of glory, may give you the Spirit of **wisdom and of revelation** in the knowledge of him, having **the eyes of your hearts enlightened,** that you may know what is **the hope** to which he has called you, what are **the riches** of his glorious inheritance in the saints, and what is the **immeasurable greatness of his power** toward us who believe, according to the working of his great might that he worked in Christ when he raised him from the dead and seated him at his right hand in the heavenly places, far above all rule and authority and power and dominion, and above every name that is named, not only in this age but also in the one to come. And he put all things under his feet and gave him as head over all things to the*

church, which is his body, the fullness of him who fills all in all.

(Ephesians 1:17–23)

HAVING THE EYES OF YOUR HEART ENLIGHTENED

When the eyes of your heart are enlightened, you cannot remain the same! God Himself is going to open your spiritual heart's eyes to see Him and your calling as it really is. He longs for you to learn what it means to walk on ground that you have prayed over, to show up every day relying on the promises you just read and learning to act upon them in the power of His Holy Spirit.

> *When they could not find them, they dragged Jason and some of the brothers before the city authorities, shouting, "These men who have turned the world upside down have come here."* (Acts 17:6)

What a way to have your life described—world changers turning things upside down. Wow! No matter how they were sharing the gospel, it had to be in the power of God's Holy Spirit!

In 1 Corinthians 4:20, the apostle Paul declares that the power of Christians is not in their talk, but in the power of the Spirit of God. I want to share this with you in four different versions.

- NLT: *"For the Kingdom of God is not just a lot of talk; it is living by God's power."*

- ESV: *"For the kingdom of God does not consist in talk but in power."*

- NIV: *"For the kingdom of God is not a matter of talk but of power."*

- KJV: *"For the kingdom of God is not in word, but in power."*

"From his innermost being will flow rivers of living water" (John 7:38 NASB). I believe the authorities who met these disciples saw, felt, and

heard this power. These world changers had such a passion, it was completely undeniable and unstoppable because it was God's power and not theirs.

This is probably one of the main reasons you decided to go on this prayer journey—you want God's power, His overflowing rivers in your life. That is why we felt led by God to write this book. You can have as much of God as you want; God desires that for you. He is longing for His bride, His church, to seek His face before they seek His hand. Through prayer and reading God's Word, this twenty-one-day journey will give you a true understanding that Christianity—your love for Jesus—is real and powerful, not just a lot of talk.

> *Learning about prayer and its precious gift to us, its function in our lives, and the life-changing power it provides will transform your life forever!*

Learning about prayer and its precious gift to us, its function in our lives, and the life-changing power it provides will transform your life forever! I'm not a preacher, not a pastor; I have no ministry degree. I'm a normal Christian guy who is also a businessman. For me, this powerful gift of prayer from God is the biggest life-changer in my Christian walk! I know that spending these days before almighty God, worshipping Him, ministering to Him, honoring Him, and magnifying Him, perhaps in ways unfamiliar to you, will open the eyes of your understanding and permit you to go deeper with Him.

Of course, when you gave your life to Jesus Christ to be your Savior, the Holy Spirit took up residence in your life and you became a Christian. But have you consistently had an intimate relationship with Him, one where He moves with the awesome power of living waters flowing through you into the lives of the people around you? no

Would you like to know Him this way? Would you like to experience God more intimately than you ever thought possible? I believe that God wants you to experience Him more deeply and wants you to live the abundant, extraordinary life that He promised us. Jesus said, *"I came that they may have life and have it abundantly"* (John 10:10). And we're not talking about what the world considers abundance, which is more *stuff*.

Acts 4:13 says, *"Now when they saw the boldness of Peter and John, and perceived that they were uneducated, common men, they were astonished. And they recognized that they had been with Jesus."* The Jewish council realized these guys were not Pharisees, Sadducees, or even rabbis. They were blown away because the awesome presence of the Holy Spirit rested on these two uneducated fishermen who were just ordinary guys who happened to hang out with Jesus! They knew the power of Jesus had spilled over to and upon them to make them so knowledgeable and bold.

Well, if you're ready to go to the next level in your Christian life, then hang on! If you have the courage to take this three-week challenge, read the Word with us, pray with us, and believe with us that God Himself will personally shower you with His presence, then this little book is for you. Join us if you want to change—and I mean really change! You will encounter the supernatural power of almighty God so He can live in you and through you. He longs for you to experience this for yourself. God desires to transform your life into one that allows you to become the very best that God intended you to be, to take you from the daily mundane to an extraordinary life in Christ!

APART FROM JESUS, WE CAN DO NOTHING

Now, this is not a self-help book that teaches you how to *pull yourself up by your bootstraps*. We can't do anything that's spiritually vital apart from Jesus Christ; in fact, He told us so, saying, *"Apart from me you can do nothing"* (John 15:5). But He also promised us that if we put

Him first, learn to wait upon Him, and use the gifts He has given us to elevate Him in the world around us, then He would grant us His favor! He would give us His presence!

Do you realize what will happen when you commit to putting God first and spending time in His presence in prayer? God Himself, through His Word and fellowship with the Holy Spirit, will transform you right in front of those you love and those for whom you may be interceding. Everyone who knows you will see clearly that you have been changed, that you have something now that you didn't have before…and they are going to want what you have. And since God did it, He will receive all the glory. You won't even want any credit for yourself; that is the humbling nature of God's presence.

This *21 Days of Deeper Prayer* is designed so that you will learn more about the laws of the supernatural than ever before. You will learn to apply the truths of our opening Scripture in Ephesians 1:17–23 and watch how His *"unmeasurable greatness"* is demonstrated to you and the lives of people for whom you are interceding. You will experience moments that will transform you from the inside out.

You will graduate from this spiritual boot camp with more knowledge of the supernatural and how to use the tools and weapons God has given to all who call upon His Holy name. You will become more productive spiritually than ever before *if you apply these principles daily.* Your life, the life of your church, your calling, your career, your relationships—everything you do can be infused with God's power, blessing, and His presence when you learn His way, which is to seek first His kingdom and His righteousness. (See Matthew 6:33.)

You will also learn more about spiritual warfare. Putting on *"the whole armor of God"* (see Ephesians 6:11) is not just some random biblical saying. It's preparation for warfare—and if ever the church has needed warriors and true soldiers of the cross who understand how to use the weapons God gave us, it's right now. Daniel and I are glad you are here with us, so let's seek the face of God as we start our journey into *21 Days of Deeper Prayer* together.

Your brother,
Jim Maxim

Use the
Weapon of prayer
= put God first in my days

Join the Interactive
21 Days of Deeper Prayer
Experience!

To help you in this prayer journey, go online to access a daily playlist of prayers to be used along with this book.

Here's how it works:

+ Read the devotional for that day.

+ Go online and listen to the corresponding prayers for that day.

+ Pray in agreement with us for the Almighty to help you experience a deeper prayer life for His glory and for your good.

+ Share this resource with your brothers and sisters in Christ that we all might agree.

Our hope is that this will be a powerful tool to change your prayer life and help usher you in to the daily presence of God.

Visit either of these websites to hear the prayers for the day:

www.acts413.net/deeperprayer

www.strategicrenewal.com/21days-deeper-prayer

The Foundation of Prayer

Jim Maxim

Our Father in heaven, hallowed be Your name.
—Luke 11:2 (NKJV)

*Now it came to pass, as He [Jesus] was praying in a certain place,
when He ceased, that one of His disciples said to Him, "**Lord,
teach us to pray,** as John also taught his disciples." So He said to
them, "When you pray, say: Our Father in heaven, hallowed be
Your name. Your kingdom come. Your will be done on earth as it
is in heaven. Give us day by day our daily bread. And forgive us
our sins, for we also forgive everyone who is indebted to us. And
do not lead us into temptation, but deliver us from the evil one."*
—Luke 11:1–4 (NKJV)

The disciples knew Jesus went away alone to pray, sometimes for entire nights, and they witnessed His supernatural miracles and healings daily. It must have had a tremendous impact on them! Luke 11:1–4 tells us that right after the disciples watched Jesus finish another one of His prayer times, they asked Him to teach them how to pray. Do you think they recognized where Jesus's strength and power came from? Of course, they did! They realized that it came from His prayer time with the Father! Of all the things they could have asked Jesus that day, they asked Him, "Teach us to do what you just did, to pray the way you just prayed."

It reminds me of one of my sons coming to me when they were just kids after they watched me do something that they wanted to emulate. "Dad, would you show me how to do that?" What would you do with that question from your child? Would you give them the wrong answer to frustrate them? If they wanted to learn how to drive, would you just throw them the car keys without any instructions? I don't think so. I think you would give them very specific answers.

Was Jesus serious when He gave the disciples this prayer or was it just a suggestion for them to consider? Jesus was serious! He wanted the disciples to pray to the Father just as He did. And He wants us to do the same—to pray the way that He prayed—what we call *The Lord's Prayer*. Jesus wants us to look at the steps that He followed as He went to His Father. *This is the very foundation of prayer.* Jesus wanted His disciples and the church to understand how we should speak to the Father, how we should approach almighty God in order to enter into His holy presence.

In the next prayer days, we'll look at how Jesus's prayer example sets the foundation for our deeper walk with Him.

"OUR FATHER IN HEAVEN..."

The first words Jesus spoke were *"Our Father."* He wanted to ensure that He truly is our Father and that we have surrendered our life to the God who loves us. When Jesus said *"Our Father"* to His disciples, He was not talking to those who did not have God as their Father. God wants to be certain that He is *our* Father as well; His desire to show us His love is the reason He sent Jesus into the world.

Of course, God still hears the cry of a sinner. He hears the cry of those who are lost when they call out to Him for help. Thank God, He heard my cry when I was not saved. But He knew that my heart's true desire was to have Him as my Father. I just didn't know how to get there.

Take a moment to ask yourself, "Is God my Father today?" If He is not, then now is the time to make Him your Father. If you have never bowed your heart to Jesus Christ and personally asked Him to forgive you and cleanse you of your sin, we can start right here. Say this prayer with me:

> Almighty God, in the holy name of Jesus, I come to You, and I ask You to forgive me and to cleanse me of all of my sin. Lord Jesus, I bow before You and I acknowledge that I am a sinner. Please forgive me and come to live in my life; please be the Lord of my life. I want to be in Your family. Jesus, I give you my heart today; help me to serve You and to worship You. I surrender everything to You.

"HALLOWED BE YOUR NAME..."

We acknowledge that God is our Father. Then Jesus tells us we are to *hallow* the God of the universe and His name—that means to reverence, worship, honor, and adore Him. Jesus reverenced His Father, and we need to do the same!

> *While Jesus was here on earth, he offered prayers and pleadings, with a loud cry and tears, to the one who could rescue him from death.* **And God heard his prayers because of his deep reverence for God.**   (Hebrews 5:7 NLT)

I don't want you to miss this: *God heard Jesus's prayers because Jesus had a deep reverence for His Father.*

My desire during these prayer days is for you to learn the powerful secrets of praying to our heavenly Father. We want God to answer our prayers, but we should also want to know *why* God will answer our prayers. Giving Him reverence as Jesus did is a big part of receiving those answers. It's a foundational truth that you should not approach God casually without the reverence He deserves. Casual prayer is a mistake. I want to repeat that. *Casual prayer is a mistake!* I'm not saying we should be too afraid of God to approach Him. I am saying that we need to have the biblical fear that is defined as reverence for the God of the universe. Jesus gave His Father reverence and because Jesus did so, *"God heard his prayers."*

> *We need to have the biblical fear that is defined as reverence for the God of the universe.*

How often do you take sixty or even thirty minutes just to minister to almighty God? How do you hallow or honor Him? What does this look like? You can open your heart and mind to the Almighty and bow in His presence. Confess His Holiness. Honor Him, worship Him, and magnify Him. Confess your sin to Him. Place Him on the throne of your life and humble yourself in His presence. He alone is the Most High God, and He alone is worthy. Worship Him with the words of your mouth, bless Him, and bow before Him. This is hallowing, honoring, and extoling God Almighty.

When I understood how much Jesus reverenced His Father, I began to pray the Lord's Prayer from my heart. To make it more real to me, I developed a personal way to express my reverence. While I'm in my prayer closet, sometimes I will place a small towel over my left arm and pray, "Lord, will you please allow me to wash Your feet with my spirit today? I humble myself before You, I bow before you, almighty God." This is not some kind of formula I'm suggesting you do. It's just a simple way *for me* to humble myself before God.

Why would I do this? I do it for several reasons:

+ First, the God of the universe is altogether worthy. That's the number one reason. God is worthy of all our praise and adoration.

+ Second, His holiness demands our attitude of reverence. I use the towel to remind myself that I am completely and utterly dependent upon God. I do this to get my spirit reverent before God the Father. We should humble ourselves in the posture that His holiness requires. Reverence is a prerequisite in prayer. Why are some people effective and others are not? Why does James tell us, *"The effective prayer of a righteous man* [or woman] *can accomplish much"* (James 5:16 NASB)? The attitude of your heart, the attitude of your being, and the attitude of your soul must align with humility.

+ Third, Satan goes before God to condemn us. (See Revelation 12:10.) I worship God to make a statement to the demonic world that is attacking my mind and telling me, "I'm a loser," or "I will never amount to anything," or other negative thoughts that come to mind. When I declare God's holiness and I declare His reverence and His majesty, it tears down the wicked thoughts and ugly spirits that are against me. Just like prayer, praise to almighty God is one of our greatest weapons. My praise solves so many issues when I acknowledge God for who He is. *"Praise the LORD! Blessed is the man who fears* [reverences] *the LORD, who greatly delights in his commandments!"* (Psalm 112:1).

My friends, in order to have the very best relationship with God—the one for which He created you, the relationship you long for—you must understand that *He is holy.* You must give Him the reverence, the honor, the glory, and the majesty that are due His name.

Today we are going to do that together. Let's go to God right now and show Him our reverence and gratitude. Let's seek His face without even wanting to seek His hand, and show the Lord that we willingly acknowledge His Holiness, majesty, beauty, and sovereignty over all mankind.

Join us for prayer on Day 1 at:

www.acts413.net/deeperprayer
OR
www.strategicrenewal.com/21days-deeper-prayer

Day 2

As It Is in Heaven

Jim Maxim

Your kingdom come.
Your will be done on earth as it is in heaven.
—Luke 11:2 (NKJV)

Can you picture meeting God in heaven seated on His throne with Jesus Christ and the Holy Spirit standing right in front of you? Don't you think you would fall on your face and bow as low as you possibly could to show *Them*, the Trinity, just how much you love, honor, and respect Them?

Why should it be any different right now as we live on earth?

I believe that one of the main reasons Christians today don't desire to pray the way the disciples did is that we don't really see the Father, Son, and Holy Spirit the way we should, who They really are in Their power and majesty in heaven.

> *Yours, O Lord, is the greatness and the power and the glory and the victory and the majesty, for all that is in the heavens and in the earth is yours. Yours is the kingdom, O Lord, and you are exalted as head above all.* (1 Chronicles 29:11)

[God's] immeasurable greatness of his power toward us who believe, according to the working of his great might that he worked in Christ when he raised him from the dead and seated him at his right hand in the heavenly places, far above all rule and authority and power and dominion, and above every name that is named, not only in this age but also in the one to come.

(Ephesians 1:19–21)

When Jesus was teaching the disciples how to pray, He wanted them to understand the kingdom of God in heaven could be brought down to earth in their prayers. The disciples *saw* Jesus pray to a heavenly Father and then they *saw* what Jesus did from there. They knew He had received power, confidence, faith, and renewed ability from the time He spent with His Father. It can be the same for us! = me

"YOUR KINGDOM COME..."

In order to grow in our faith and have our prayers answered, what does Jesus tell us? *"Seek first the kingdom of God and his righteousness, and all these things will be added to you"* (Matthew 6:33). What does it mean to seek the kingdom of God? It means seeking God's face before I seek God's hand, seeking God's face by waiting before Him in His presence, respecting Him, and reverencing Him. It means caring more about having a relationship with almighty God than worrying about what He is going to *do for me* next, even though the verse also says that He will provide for what we need.

"YOUR WILL BE DONE..."

In today's English that means, "God, I want it Your way no matter what!" I know you are reading through this book because you want to go to the next level in your relationship with God. You really want to say to Him, *"Not my will, but Your will, almighty God."* You're on your way when this becomes your prayer of faith because you're truly believing His will is better than yours—even if it is not what you want!

That's the difference between having Jesus as your *Lord* and Savior, or just your Savior. When He is your Lord, your faith and trust in the Father, Son, and Holy Spirit leads you to surrender the decisions of your life to Him. Now, I'm not saying that this is always the easiest decision. For me, it takes all my pride and ego and puts it aside because He is Lord and God; it is His will that must be done, not mine.

"ON EARTH AS IT IS IN HEAVEN…"

Do you think much about heaven? When you do, what comes to mind? Is it seeing God Almighty seated on the throne of heaven with Jesus at His right hand? What does heaven really look like and what goes on there? There are certain things that we know according to God's Word. Many scenes in the Bible describe the throne room of God, the angels, and the heavenly creatures who cry without ceasing, *"Holy, holy, holy, is the Lord God Almighty"* (Revelation 4:8). We know there are twenty-four elders seated around the throne of God who fall to their knees crying, *"Worthy are you, our Lord and God, to receive glory and honor and power"* (Revelation 4:11). Some of these descriptions seem strange to us as we go about life on earth, but they set the stage for recognizing God's holiness and His supernatural power.

Psalm 46:4 gives us an additional picture of heaven: *"There is a river whose streams make glad the city of God."* What river is that? It is the river of life that flows from the throne of God Almighty! The apostle John wrote, *"Then the angel showed me the river of the water of life, bright as crystal, flowing from the throne of God and of the Lamb through the middle of the street of the city"* (Revelation 22:1–2). This is the river of God's power, God's love, and God's majesty. It's this river flowing from heaven's throne that Jesus was referring to when He said, *"From his innermost being will flow rivers of living water"* (John 7:38 NASB). The river that gives us these living waters has its beginning in heaven!

Jesus was giving us the secret to living a victorious life with the words *"on earth as it is in heaven"* from the Lord's Prayer. He was encouraging us to look into the spiritual world first and see how things are done in heaven. He was declaring that this world is subject to heaven's authority. Remember this verse, *"Jesus came and said to them, 'All authority in heaven and on earth has been given to me'"* (Matthew 28:18). Then Jesus ascended to His Father to be seated at God's right hand forever, *"far above all rule and authority and power and dominion"* (Ephesians 1:21).

Reading these words leads me to pray:

Dear God, please forgive us for not seeing Your majesty. God, please forgive our lack of faith. Father, in the name of Jesus, please help us to see You as You truly are. Help us to see things on earth as it is in heaven.

Ask yourself a couple of questions. Can God's will truly be done on earth as it is in heaven? Would Jesus have said this if it were not true? Why would Jesus want us to have this mindset that God's will can be done on earth as it is in heaven? Perhaps it's because He knew we didn't understand how to pray, that the motivation of our hearts might be right, but we still hadn't considered our approach to God. Jesus knew that to pray with the mindset *"as it is in heaven"* was foundational to our prayer life. If we get this wrong, all our praying could be amiss.

Jesus knew that to pray with the mindset "as it is in heaven" was foundational to our prayer life.

In heaven, God's will is the only will considered. In heaven, God's supernatural power is revealed. As Christians, we should believe it can be the same way on earth. Jesus is waiting for us to pray the way He told the disciples to pray when they asked Him. I believe that our walk with Jesus can be so much more. I believe that we can experience the overflowing *"rivers of living water"* that He promised us when we recognize God for who He is and truly believe that our prayers will be answered when we ask Him to let things on earth be *"as it is in heaven."*

My brothers and sisters, today let's ask God to help us believe in Him and see things as they truly are in heaven. Please join us for prayer on Day 2 at:

www.acts413.net/deeperprayer
OR
www.strategicrenewal.com/21days-deeper-prayer

Day 5

Life as He Intended

Jim Maxim

*How precious to me are your thoughts, O God! How vast is
the sum of them! If I would count them, they are more than the
sand. I awake, and I am still with you.*
—Psalm 139:17–18

God created You to live life the way He intended. You are unique.
You are essential. You are *"the apple of* [God's] *eye"* (Psalm 17:8). You
are His child, His creation. You are the desire of His heart. You are
beautiful in His sight. Yes, *you*. You are His child, His son, His daughter,
part of His royal family. He chose you.

> *You did not choose me, but I chose you and appointed you that
> you should go and bear fruit and that your fruit should abide, so
> that whatever you ask the Father in my name, he may give it to
> you.* (John 15:16)

You are a bearer of fruit! Everywhere you go, you carry the
life-giving presence of almighty God. Look at why He chose you:
"That you would go and bear fruit, and that your fruit would remain"

(John 15:16 NASB). That's the real you, that's the son or daughter God created you to be. He longs for you to *let Him live big in your life*. But as Jesus said, you can't do it alone.

> *Abide in Me, and I in you. As the branch cannot bear fruit of itself, unless it abides in the vine, neither can you, unless you abide in Me.*   (John 15:4 NKJV)

Let's pray these two prayers daily, among others:

Father God, please don't let me limit You in my mind. Father, please take the lid off of my thinking and allow me to think the thoughts You have towards me. Please, God, help me to walk in the path You have for me to bring You glory and for the sake of the gospel.

Father, please use me to make faith come alive in someone's heart somewhere today. Please, God, help me to be sensitive to those around me, to shower Your love and hope upon them, to bring them to the saving knowledge of Jesus Christ for Your eternal glory.

God longs for you to grow in Him and to become the best *you* possible. I know you feel that same longing in the deepest part of your soul. The body of Christ is better when the real you shows up. We, the body of Christ, need the real you. Your world needs the real you.

During His earthly ministry, *"Jesus stood and cried out, saying, 'If anyone thirsts, let him come to Me and drink. He who believes in Me, as the Scripture has said, out of his heart will flow rivers of living water"* (John 7:37–38 NKJV).

The burden I have for God's people is that they would get *unstuck* from a mundane or routine Christian life and embrace what God

Almighty has for them—what His plan for them will mean for their lives right now, what His plan will mean for their families, and how it would affect the world around them. Our lives become *unstuck* when we understand God's desire for us. This book was written with a passion for you, as a Christian, to walk more closely with God Almighty and to become the *real you* that God intended you to be. When we begin to focus first on the kingdom of heaven and our true desire is to do His will, then and only then will real contentment, peace, and supernatural power flow naturally from our lives.

Now, this is not meant to be a way to get all the things that you want or elevate yourself in the eyes of the world. The purpose is to become the *you* God always had in mind, for His kingdom and His glory. In the end, it is all about God and His kingdom goals. And He is the One who will bring it to pass—not us!

We read Jesus's words: *"Apart from me you* [little you] *can do nothing"* (John 15:5). But He also said, *"You, the real you, can do all things through Christ who strengthens you."* (See Philippians 4:13.) In other words, Jesus is saying, "If you do it My way, if you let Me work in you, I will flow out of you and through you every single day of your life, and the real you will show up!"

> *To become the person God intended you to be, you must do it the way He intended you to do it, with His Word and His power!*

The apostle Paul put it this way:

I have been crucified with Christ. It is no longer I who live, but Christ who lives in me. And the life that I now live in the flesh I

> live by faith in the Son of God, who loved me and gave himself for
> me.   (Galatians 2:20)

So what power are we trying to use in this life? In God's reality, to become the person God intended you to be, you must do it *the way He intended you to do it*, with His Word and His power! Jesus said, *"I am the vine; you are the branches. Those who remain in me, and I in them, will produce much fruit. For apart from me you can do nothing"* (John 15:5 NLT). And He meant exactly what He said! Apart from Him, we can't do it! But with His leading, by the power of the Holy Spirit, He can transform our Christian lives into a life of power in Him. So He promises, *"rivers of living water"* (John 7:38). Living waters for you, your family and friends, and the world around you that is dying without a Savior. Waters that will bring life to any situation through the gateway of prayer.

These days of prayer were designed so that you will learn how to pray to a God who hears and answers you. You will experience these moments with almighty God that will transform you and your understanding of the spiritual world. With the apostle Paul, *"I pray that the eyes of your heart may be enlightened"* (Ephesians 1:18 NIV), that you will know, see, taste, and feel the power of the Holy Spirit in prayer, and learn how to bring others with you before God by praying the Scriptures.

Now, let's go to the throne room together and pray.

Join us in prayer for Day 3 at:

www.acts413.net/deeperprayer
OR
www.strategicrenewal.com/21days-deeper-prayer

Holy Spirit, You Are Welcome

Jim Maxim

The priests could not continue their service because of the cloud, for
the glorious presence of the Lord filled the Temple of the Lord.
—1 Kings 8:11 (NLT)

Do you know what touches me so much about this verse? I see these Old Testament priests as a representation of you and me today. I see men and women who are called by God to worship Him, serve Him, and take care of His people. I'm sure that most of these priests had tender hearts for God, and they probably stayed very busy in their daily services to Him.

I'm sure that you are a lot like that. I'm sure you have been dedicated in your service to the Lord. Yet, deep down you know there is something more, a deeper awareness of who God is or who He can be in your life, a deeper longing in your soul that you know God has placed there. In some ways, our desire for God will never be completely satisfied while we live on this earth. But He wants us to search for a closer relationship with Him until we finally see Him face to face.

> *The priests could not continue their service because of the cloud,*
> *for the glorious presence of the* LORD *filled the Temple of the*
> LORD.   (1 Kings 8:11 NLT)

This verse is a beautiful example of how God wants so much more in our relationship with Him. God is always with us, but some days, He just stops us in our tracks to allow us to experience Him in a new way that completely drenches us with Himself. God permits us to *feel* Him more, *love* Him more, *understand* Him more, and on and on.

I cannot describe all that happens when a liquid sea, an overpowering wave of God's love, washes over you and doesn't stop until you are completely undone, bowing at His feet in awe. Nothing in this world can come close to the experience of God's presence dwelling with you personally. The Holy Spirit Himself fills the room and you don't want to move because of the indwelling of His holiness resting upon every fiber of your being. You know the only right thing to do is to receive this gift and respond to Him by saying, "You are holy, holy, holy," just as the heavenly creatures cry before God's throne in heaven. (See Revelation 4:8.)

> *Experiencing the presence of God is unusual and*
> *supernatural because He is the God of all creation!*

I realize that some people may be concerned that this is a little *out there* or *weird*. You know, the definition of weird includes words like *unnatural*, *supernatural*, *mysterious*, and *unusual*. Well, experiencing the presence of God *is* unusual and supernatural because He is the God of all creation! It doesn't mean we don't still lead our productive lives. Remember, I'm a Christian who happens to be called to the business world. I have a plan; I seek guidance from attorneys, financial experts, and marketing professionals; I use the best technology; and I employ the most talented people I can find. But I also welcome the presence and guidance of the Holy Spirit in every area of my life. Remember, Jesus said to His disciples, *"Nevertheless, I tell you the truth: it is to your advantage that I go away, for if I do not go away, the Helper will not come to you. But if I go, I will send him to you"* (John 16:7).

God sent the Holy Spirit to be with us always as believers. Shouldn't our lives as Christians—pilgrims in the world and children of the Most High God—experience God's presence like this? Shouldn't we be able to have such intimate times with our heavenly Father? The presence of the Holy Spirit will make us more aware that we have been redeemed and that our lives are truly *"hidden with Christ in God"* (Colossians 3:3).

What would one of our church services look like today if God's presence were to fill the sanctuary as it did with the priests in the temple? Would we welcome Him, the Holy Spirit? Would we even know what to do if this happened? Would we be willing to *stop everything and wait upon Him* to see what *He* wanted to do? (See Psalm 27:14.)

Maybe you have forgotten about the *true power* of God that comes from the Holy Spirit in our lives. Jesus reassures us, *"But you will receive power when the Holy Spirit has come upon you, and you will be my witnesses in Jerusalem and in all Judea and Samaria, and to the end of the earth"* (Acts 1:8). Maybe you once relied upon God's power, but somehow you have slowly shifted to *your* power, *your* ego, and *your* effort. Maybe you plan every detail of your life and ministry without going to God for His guidance and infilling. There must be a time in your walk with God when you honestly realize that unless it's God's power and not yours, it will never last.

Well, you can start all over again right now. At this moment, Christ can baptize you afresh with the Holy Spirit, flow through you once again, and use you to change lives like He really wants to do.

Jesus longs to use people who are fully surrendered to His love and His power. Jesus will cleanse you and forgive you, and He can make it all new for you again. Just ask Him right now to forgive you and guide you, and He will fill you to overflowing. Out of your innermost being will flow *"rivers of living water"* (John 7:38). Go ahead and ask Him right now.

Earlier, I promised you that if you stayed with us for twenty-one days that your life would be changed for God's glory and your productivity, peace, and contentment. How can I make this promise? Because right now, we are going to experience God's holy, life-changing presence together. Today, right now, you are going to experience His supernatural love.

Today will be an extended time of prayer, so let's go together to Him and call upon His Holy and majestic name. Let's seek His wonderful face before we seek His all-powerful hand.

Join us for prayer on Day 4 at:

www.acts413.net/deeperprayer
OR
www.strategicrenewal.com/21days-deeper-prayer

Prayer: An Infusion of God's Tailor-Made Grace

Daniel Henderson

For from his fullness we have all received, grace upon grace.
—John 1:16

A man can no more take in a supply of grace for the future
than he can eat enough today to last him for the next six
months, nor can he inhale sufficient air into his lungs with one
breath to sustain life for a week to come. We are permitted to
draw upon God's store of grace from day to day as we need it.
—D. L. Moody

For ten days, our family sat by the hospital bed of my suffering mother. At first, a previous surgery to remove the aggressive cancer cells from her lung appeared to be successful. Soon we learned the metastasized cells had penetrated her bones. The process of her painful death moved quickly. In her final days, she lay quietly, overdosed with pain medication and laboring to breathe as she journeyed toward eternity.

The morning before her death, she suddenly opened her eyes wide and began to express the most glorious praise, continuing for over a minute with heartfelt declarations of her love and gratitude for Jesus. Our family witnessed an amazing demonstration of her fully alive spirit, transcending a rapidly failing body, to soar into the heavenlies with intimate worship of Christ. What I saw that morning could only be described as *dying grace*. The Lord was giving her a longing for His presence and an expectation of eternity's glory. As a pastor for thirty years, I've witnessed this amazing display of the tender, unmerited favor of God in the lives of many as they knocked on death's door.

What do you pray for when you don't know what to pray for? What do you seek from God when you are struggling or suffering? We can learn from the apostle Paul's experience as he begged God, three times, to remove a debilitating thorn in his flesh. His pleading eventually turned to praise, his burden changed to blessing, and his thorn gave him cause for thanks. (See 2 Corinthians 12:7–10.) Why? Because Jesus imparted a life-transforming truth and provision to Paul in the midst of his anguish: *"My grace is sufficient for you, for my power is made perfect in weakness"* (verse 9). Paul learned that Jesus responds to our affliction in prayer with amazing, divine grace.

UNIQUE, SPECIFIC, TIMELY PROVISION

The concept of God's unique provision of specific grace was first birthed in my understanding during high school during the days of the Cold War. Superpower nations threatened one another with weapons of mass destruction. Urban speculations circulated about the potential for Communists taking over our nation and putting Christians to death in a ruthless wave of persecution. Stories of this kind of thing in other nations surfaced in the news. Christian songs were even written about the future need to meet in secret for fear of maltreatment.

Periodically, I wondered, *What would I do if I were brought before a firing squad with threats to denounce my faith or die? How would I handle it? What would I say?* In time, as I clearly understood the power and practicality of grace, I gained assurance that I did not need to worry. If that moment ever came, God would lavish me with grace for a bold, glorious martyrdom in the exact instant it was needed.

EXPERIENCE GRACE. EXPECT IT!

The popular acrostic for grace, *God's Riches At Christ's Expense*, is more than a pithy slogan. The sacrifice of Christ's redemption invites us to the abundance of heaven's supply of grace for our most desperate and very practical needs. John 1:16 says that out of Christ's abundance, we have all received *"grace upon grace."* Another translation says, *"From his abundance we have all received one gracious blessing after another"* (NLT). Like the endless rhythm of ocean waves washing onto a beach, God's grace lavishes our lives with a continual provision of His supernatural enabling for our chronic limitations.

Just as we expected and experienced sufficient, converting grace when we came to Christ and were transformed by His power, so we should live with confident expectation that His provision will be enough every day. Grace is not just a past-tense salvation miracle. It is a present-tense sanctification wonder. We can live each day expecting a fresh phenomenon of grace in our lives.

RECOGNIZE GRACE. UNDERSTAND IT!

I like to define grace as "God doing *for me, in me,* and *through me* what only He can do through the person and power of Jesus Christ." This grace is not a crutch for the lazy or irresponsible. Grace works in conjunction with my conscientious efforts, not instead of them. Paul wrote of this when he said, *"But by the grace of God I am what I am, and his grace toward me was not in vain. On the contrary, I worked harder than any of them, though it was not I, but the grace of God that is with me"* (1 Corinthians 15:10). Grace meets us to do what we *cannot* do, while we do what we are *able* to do. Every effort on my part, even my prayer, is but an overflow of the constant provisions of His grace. It may sound like a riddle, but in reality, it is the two-sided coin of empowering grace.

Grace is not an escape to some leisurely world where life is safe, pressures have disappeared, and all is flowers and fun. Grace is a deliverance from the devastating powers of this world's allure and deceptions. As Paul says:

> *For the grace of God that brings salvation has appeared to all men, teaching us that, denying ungodliness and worldly lusts, we should live soberly, righteously, and godly in the present age.*
> (Titus 2:11–12 NKJV)

Do you want to see someone who understands grace? Look for the fruit of clear-minded, consecrated, Christlike behavior in their lives.

Again, all of this grace is tailor-made, flowing from the provision of our all-wise, all-sufficient God as we call on Him. In the trenches of pastoral ministry, I've witnessed extravagant displays of saving grace, guiding grace, sustaining grace, unifying grace, and suffering grace. I've marveled at specialized grace arriving—seldom early but never late. The beautiful manifestations of His undeserved enabling have supported the confused, the depressed, the broken, the troubled teen, the lonely single adult, the barren couple, the stalled marriage, the empty-nester, and the pain-afflicted senior adult. All of this is available as we pray.

HOOKED INTO A HEAVENLY IV DRIP

If you've ever been hospitalized, as I have on a few occasions, you know that one of the first and most essential medical treatments is the insertion of an intravenous (IV) tube into a major vein. This provides a means for the doctor to administer an endless variety of specialized treatments for the patient's well-being. The basic hydrating saline solution becomes the carrier for ingredients vital to healing, comfort, and nutrition.

I like to think of grace like an IV to the heart, flowing with unique and in-the-moment formulas of Christ's provision. It started to gush the moment we turned toward Christ. It supplies His full provision for all we need, regardless of the trial or temptation. Right now, as you read, it is flowing.

The basic formula in this life-giving current is the power of the Holy Spirit, applying the truth of God's Word as we pray. But the unique application can change based upon your situation. Just like a patient receives an instantly delivered formula of sustenance, so do we in Christ. And just as that formula can be supplemented with a myriad of antibiotics, pain medications, blood thinners, anti-inflammatory aids, and other drugs, so does the Lord provide exactly what we need, as we need it, and when we need it.

It really is amazing, isn't it? So, let's trust and obey the great appeal of God to come to Him and pray earnestly. As we now pray together, *"Let us then with confidence draw near to the throne of grace, that we may receive mercy and find grace to help in time of need"* (Hebrews 4:16).

Join us for prayer on Day 5 at:

www.acts413.net/deeperprayer
OR
www.strategicrenewal.com/21days-deeper-prayer

Prayer Worthy of Our Creator

Daniel Henderson

Worthy are you, our Lord and God,
to receive glory and honor and power.
—Revelation 4:11

Several times a year, we have the occasion to visit one of the world's great museums located near our home, the Denver Museum of Nature and Science. This immense building encompasses multiple floors of truly amazing displays that feature taxidermies of hundreds of creatures from around the world, a massive array of dinosaurs, thousands of samples of gems and minerals, and a fascinating array of insects and butterflies. Beyond this, the facility includes a *space odyssey* section and a separate planetarium that blows one's mind with the realities of the universe. In addition, the museum houses an IMAX theater that regularly takes viewers on captivating visual explorations of the depths of the sea, the expanse of the earth, and the wonder of the skies.

SUPPRESSING THE TRUTH

All of this is touted without a scant mention of a Creator. Rather, it is a tribute to evolution and the ingenuity of man's powers of discovery.

The truth of Romans concerning the resolve of mankind to *suppress the truth* about the Creator resounded in my mind as I took it all in:

> For what can be known about God is plain to them, because God has shown it to them. For his invisible attributes, namely, his eternal power and divine nature, have been clearly perceived, ever since the creation of the world, in the things that have been made. So they are without excuse. For although they knew God, they did not honor him as God **or give thanks to him, but they became futile in their thinking, and their foolish hearts were darkened. Claiming to be wise, they became fools.**
>
> (Romans 1:19–22)

I usually leave the museum wondering how anyone with a sense of moral conscience could reject the power of a divine cause in light of all they witnessed. Yet, the Bible makes it very clear that a denial of the Creator leads to a lack of thanksgiving toward Him, which eventually culminates in futility of thought and utter foolishness.

On the positive side, when we accept the account of Genesis 1 and thus honor our majestic Creator and His immeasurable work, we are overwhelmed with earnest gratitude for His power, beauty, fathomless plan, and divine care. This is ultimate wisdom and sanity in a world gone mad.

OUR CREATOR AND OUR PRAYERS

How does this relate to prayer? Over the years, the foundational truths of our Creator and His creative power have shaped my praying and my leadership in prayer. I teach on this extensively in the book *PRAYzing!: Creative Prayer Experiences from A to Z*[1] and expand on it in my coaching with pastors.

1. Daniel Henderson, *PRAYzing!: Creative Prayer Experiences from A to Z* (Colorado Springs, CO: NavPress, 2007).

We can be assured that God is not the author of boredom, especially when we are communing with Him. The early verses of Genesis can serve as a *boredom buster* for individual and collective prayer experiences.

The opening verses of Genesis give us great insight:

> *In the beginning, God created the heavens and the earth. The earth was without form and void, and darkness was over the face of the deep. And the Spirit of God was hovering over the face of the waters. And God said, "Let there be light," and there was light.*   (Genesis 1:1–3)

Based on these foundational truths, here are the applications that have helped me so powerfully.

We Always Pray to a Creative God

A. W. Tozer famously noted, "The most important thing about a person is what comes to mind when they think about God." Genesis 1:1 should powerfully shape our understanding of Him and of prayer. God's first explanation of Himself and first act in the history of man point to Him as Creator. Every time I lead in prayer, I am resting my confidence and anticipation in the truth that my God is absolutely creative—far beyond my limited ability to comprehend. He is not a God of dull reruns. He does not mass produce duplicates. He is infinitely and beautifully creative in all of His works.

We Can Pray by His Creative Spirit

Genesis 1:2 speaks of the Spirit of God hovering over the dark and formless waters. By the power of the Spirit, the worlds were created. Now, as a redeemed Christ-follower, I can embrace the incredible truth that the Spirit of God in Genesis 1:2 is the very Spirit that lives in me, guides my thoughts, and enlivens my heart.

Some folks might offer the excuse, "I don't have a creative bone in my body." Thankfully, praying and leading in prayer is not about *bones* but rather about the indwelling Spirit of the Creator who guides our minds and leads our prayers. The Scriptures affirm this.

> But, as it is written, "What no eye has seen, nor ear heard, nor the heart of man imagined, what God has prepared for those who love him"— these things God has revealed to us through the Spirit. For the Spirit searches everything, even the depths of God.
>
> (1 Corinthians 2:9–10)

We Should Pray from His Creative Word

"*And God said…*" (Genesis 1:3). This was the spark of creation, His powerful Word punctuating the entire creation story. Today, our creativity in prayer is fueled not simply by our meager thoughts but by the power and wonder of His Word, found in the Scriptures. I always begin my prayer time, and every prayer time I lead, from the Bible. This allows the Creator to start and guide the prayer conversation, leading to true alignment with His will and a deep transformation of mind and heart.

We Were Made to Pray in a Creative Way

Later, in Genesis 2:19–20, we see that God tasks Adam with naming all the animals. Think about that. How many animals? How long did this take? How much creativity had God placed in Adam to allow the first man to accomplish this task?

When we pray, we need to rest in God's design that we were made to be creative. This is far beyond some pithy cleverness or attempt to be *original* in our human wisdom. Rather, it is the full experience of our creative God and His design for the fullness of our God-given potential in knowing and enjoying Him. Sleepy, dull, lifeless, and lackluster prayer is not worthy of the Creator or our Lord Jesus Christ, who has redeemed us and through whom the worlds were made. (See 1 Corinthians 1:30; John 1:1–3; Colossians 1:16–17.)

I think the next time I tour that remarkable museum, I will again be amazed in the presence of the all-powerful Creator. Hopefully, I will have new and compelling motivation to seek Him, because through the finished work of His Son on the cross, I can access the holy of holies and embrace the power of His indwelling presence to enjoy transforming communion with Him. Yes, this motivates me to seek Him with biblical expectation and life-giving experiences in believing prayer.

So, let's call out to our glorious Creator together as we pray now.

Join us for prayer on Day 6 at:

www.acts413.net/deeperprayer
OR
www.strategicrenewal.com/21days-deeper-prayer

One Extraordinary Day

Jim Maxim

And he [Jesus] said,
"He who has ears to hear, let him hear."
—Mark 4:9

Just one day, twelve short hours, changed the lives of Jesus's disciples forever. That one day, they experienced a surging crowd, a mesmerizing farmer's tale, a terrifying storm, a prisoner suffering from mental illness and demons, and a herd of screaming pigs.

In the next few prayer days, we'll look at how Jesus trains the disciples (and us) to have a deeper faith. Let's begin by the Sea of Galilee, where Jesus sits in a fisherman's boat in front of a large crowd, relating the story of a farmer sowing seeds.

> *Listen! Behold, a sower went out to sow. And as he sowed, some seed fell along the path, and the birds came and devoured it. Other seed fell on rocky ground, where it did not have much soil, and immediately it sprang up, since it had no depth of soil. And when the sun rose, it was scorched, and since it had no root, it withered away. Other seed fell among thorns, and the thorns grew up and*

choked it, and it yielded no grain. And other seeds fell into good soil and produced grain, growing up and increasing and yielding thirtyfold and sixtyfold and a hundredfold.… He who has ears to hear, let him hear.　　　　　　　　　　　　　(Mark 4:3–9)

This story has a sower, some seeds, and four different kinds of soil. But the story isn't about the sower and it isn't about the seeds; it's about the soil and why only one type of soil produces a harvest.

First of all, the seed, which represents God's Word, isn't to blame for harvest failure because it can't control where it's sown. The sower—the evangelist, the Christian sharing his faith—isn't to blame either; his job is just to sow the seed of God's Word. So, what's to blame for the seeds that never produce a harvest? It's the soil—my soil, your soil—the soil of our hearts. This is how Jesus explains the four different soils to His disciples and to us.

- **Soil 1.** Some seed fell along the path. *"These are the ones along the path, where the word is sown: when they hear, Satan immediately comes and takes away the word that is sown in them"* (Mark 4:15). There was no soil here, just a few grains of dirt lying on the pathway.

- **Soil 2.** Other seed fell on rocky ground and had no root, so it withered away. *"And these are the ones sown on rocky ground: the ones who, when they hear the word, immediately receive it with joy. And they have no root in themselves, but endure for a while; then, when tribulation or persecution arises on account of the word, immediately they fall away"* (Mark 4:16–17). This soil is thin without enough nutrients to grow any roots.

- **Soil 3.** Other seed fell among thorns and never produced any harvest. *"And others are the ones sown among thorns. They are those who hear the word, but the cares of the world and the deceitfulness of riches and the desires for other things enter in and choke the word,* *and it proves unfruitful"* (Mark 4:18–19). There is soil here, but it's so full of thorns—personal sin, greed, and worldly ambitions—that the seeds can't grow.

+ **Soil 4.** Other seeds fell on rich soil and produced a great, ever-increasing harvest. *"But those that were sown on the good soil are the ones who hear the word and accept it and bear fruit, thirtyfold and sixtyfold and a hundredfold"* (Mark 4:20). Thirtyfold, sixtyfold, a hundredfold! This is rich, cultivated soil that bears a great harvest for God's kingdom.

Here is the point of Jesus's lesson for the disciples then and for us now. The soil represents the hearts of people and the seed is God's Word. If our hearts are not ready for God, the seed of His Word will perish. If our hearts are cultivated and prepared, we will have the fourth kind of soil, the seed will grow, and we will be fruitful for God's kingdom. It's our choice. So, let's ask ourselves, what kind of soil do I have in my heart to receive the seed of God's Word? Am I preparing that soil so I will grow? Do I spend time enriching that soil with God Almighty's presence in prayer and with His Word? Nothing takes the place of spending time in prayer in the presence of God.

Our growth is dependent on the soil of our hearts. Where you choose to plant your beliefs about God Almighty is the determining factor of where your life will go. The soil of your thought life, the garden of your hopes and dreams, your spiritual wisdom, knowledge, and understanding of His thoughts toward you—all of these will produce greater fruit for God's kingdom in your life and bring Him glory. *"By this my Father is glorified, that you bear much fruit and so prove to be my disciples"* (John 15:8). I want to be the type of soil that yields one hundredfold! I know you do, too. You're following these devotions because you want to grow deeper and richer in the Lord.

Jesus taught His disciples about kingdom fruit and power, sometimes through a parable, other times with real-world experiences. This extraordinary day in Jesus's life that we read in the gospel of Mark is no different. He was preparing His disciples to experience the importance of having rich, deep soil…but they didn't get it yet. They didn't realize that this entire day was an object lesson for a deeper walk with the Master. Jesus was setting the stage for the extraordinary things that would be accomplished that day and for the rest of their lives.

Let's pray together now that the soil of your heart will be rich for God's Word and produce an abundant harvest in your life.

Go to our interactive prayer site for Day 7 at:

www.acts413.net/deeperprayer
OR
www.strategicrenewal.com/21days-deeper-prayer

Day 8

Let's Go to the Other Side

Jim Maxim

He [Jesus] said to them,
"Let us go across to the other side."
—Mark 4:35

It is now early evening in Jesus's extraordinary day. After He finishes explaining the story of the seed and the different kinds of soil, Jesus turns to His disciples and basically says, "All right, guys, let's go across to the other side of the lake."

I bet those disciples were feeling pretty good about themselves by then. Jesus had just taken them into His confidence, sharing the true meaning of His parable. I can imagine them giving each other *high fives* because they were going to the other side of the Sea of Galilee with Jesus while the crowd stayed behind. It's a good day with the Teacher! Little do they know they are about to get a powerful life application of Jesus's soil lesson.

How many times has this happened to us? We hear a great sermon or have an incredible time in devotions, but it doesn't dawn on us that Jesus is preparing us to apply the principles of heaven to our lives. Jesus knew when the disciples got into that boat with Him that their lives would never be the same, and they would truly understand the importance of having roots that go deep into the soil of their hearts.

> *On that day, when evening had come, he said to them, "Let us go across to the other side." And leaving the crowd, they took him with them in the boat, just as he was. And other boats were with him. And a great windstorm arose, and the waves were breaking into the boat, so that the boat was already filling. But he was in the stern, asleep on the cushion. And they woke him and said to him, "Teacher, do you not care that we are perishing?" And he awoke and rebuked the wind and said to the sea, "Peace! Be still!" And the wind ceased, and there was a great calm. He said to them, "Why are you so afraid? Have you still no faith?" And they were filled with great fear and said to one another, "Who then is this, that even the wind and the sea obey him?"* (Mark 4:35–41)

The day has suddenly taken a turn for the worst! The disciples, many of them fishermen, are panic-stricken, terrified that they are about to die in the intense storm. They knew the lake; they knew what was happening around them. Why is the Master sleeping? Why doesn't He even care? In fear and probably with some anger, the wave-drenched men cry out, *"Teacher, do you not care that we are perishing?"* If you care, why would you let this happen?

Good question. Why *did* Jesus let the storm happen and not stop it sooner?

Remember, the whole point of the soil and the seed was that Jesus wanted to *take the boys* over to the battlefield. It was time for them to personally experience the importance of the Word being firmly planted in the soil of their hearts. We know that God doesn't do anything without a reason. I can tell you unequivocally that God never wastes anything in our lives! The disciples had to learn that storms play a vital role in going to the next level with Jesus.

> *The storms of life are the fertilizers that activate the seed of God's Word in us.*

The storms of life are the fertilizers that activate the seed of God's Word in us, the seed of faith to believe that God is there for us. *"If God is for us, who can be against us?"* (Romans 8:31). In spite of their fear and lack of faith, Jesus has the whole thing under control.

Brothers and sisters, I believe God has been working in you to bring you to this point—desiring to go to the other side with Jesus. *Now is the time.* Isn't that what moving in the extraordinary with Christ is all about—going to the other side from where you are to where you really want to be? Changing and growing from the person you are to the person who is the *real you?* Getting to a deeper level in our walk with Jesus? It's time to *get in the boat with Jesus.* It's a change, and change can seem risky and scary.

God has placed a desire deep in our hearts that will never be truly satisfied until we accept His purpose for us—for His glory. If I know anything about God, it's this: His love for His family, His children, is deeper, wider, longer, and bigger than anything we ever imagined. The apostle Paul prayed that we *"being rooted and established in love, may have power, together with all the Lord's holy people, to grasp how wide and long and high and deep is the love of Christ, and to know this love that surpasses knowledge—that [we] may be filled to the measure of all the fullness of God"* (Ephesians 3:17–19 NIV).

When you realize the depth of God's love for you and have confidence in it, then you will be able to truly trust Him for the next steps. Confidence in God can only come from being with Him in prayer; there are no shortcuts to spending time with almighty God. God has a purpose for our lives, just as He did for the disciples. If we are willing to seek Him and ask Him for the wisdom to see that purpose, He will make it crystal clear to us. You are on the shore reading this today because Jesus is inviting you to get in the boat with Him. God will take you to a deeper level simply because you have decided to finally go to the other side with Jesus.

Join us in a time of prayer now as we go to the Lord for the faith to get in the boat with Jesus.

For prayer on Day 8, go to:

www.acts413.net/deeperprayer
OR
www.strategicrenewal.com/21days-deeper-prayer

Day 9

What's Waiting There?

Jim Maxim

And when Jesus had stepped out of the boat, immediately there
met him out of the tombs a man...
—Mark 5:2

Jesus and His disciples have one more challenge to face on this extraordinary day! As the boat approaches the opposite shore of the lake, the disciples are pretty shaken. Even after the storm passes, they are still frightened and now wondering, *"Who then is this, that even the wind and the sea obey him?"* (Mark 4:41). They just begin to settle down, thinking they can't wait to get out of the boat on the other side. They have no idea what Jesus has prepared just ahead of them. What could possibly happen next?

Jesus wasn't finished with the lessons for that day. Remember, the whole point of the soil and the seed was that Jesus wanted to *take the boys* over to the battlefield. It was time to personally experience the importance of the Word being firmly planted in the soil of their hearts. They needed to face two powerful battles; the first one was the storm and now it was time to meet the most demon-possessed man in Bible history!

They came to the other side of the sea, to the country of the Gerasenes. And when Jesus had stepped out of the boat, immediately there met him out of the tombs a man with an unclean spirit. He lived among the tombs. And no one could bind him anymore, not even with a chain.… Night and day among the tombs and on the mountains, he was always crying out and cutting himself with stones. And when he saw Jesus from afar, he ran and fell down before him. And crying out with a loud voice, he said, "What have you to do with me, Jesus, Son of the Most High God? I adjure you by God, do not torment me." For he was saying to him, "Come out of the man, you unclean spirit!" And Jesus asked him, "What is your name?" He replied, "My name is Legion, for we are many." And he begged him earnestly not to send them out of the country. Now a great herd of pigs was feeding there on the hillside, and they begged him, saying, "Send us to the pigs; let us enter them." So he gave them permission. And the unclean spirits came out and entered the pigs; and the herd, numbering about two thousand, rushed down the steep bank into the sea and drowned in the sea. The herdsmen fled and told it in the city and in the country. And people came to see what it was that had happened. And they came to Jesus and saw the demon-possessed man, the one who had had the legion, sitting there, clothed and in his right mind, and they were afraid.   (Mark 5:1–15)

The men who tended those pigs had just witnessed the supernatural power of Jesus and saw the demon-possessed man transformed right before their eyes! It was too much for them to handle, so in fear, they ran and brought some other people back to beg Jesus to just go away! (See Mark 5:16–17.)

What about the disciples during all this time? Can you imagine what they are thinking? Can you picture their faces? After almost capsizing in a violent storm, they are totally drenched. The *peaceful* day with the Master is a dim memory. They arrived on the *safe* shore only to witness this demon-possessed guy who is naked, breaking chains, running among tombstones, and screaming for Jesus to leave him alone. They must have been looking at each other and wondering, *Why did we get in the boat with Jesus anyway?*

That is an important question we all need to ask ourselves. Do I still want to go deeper with God? Am I sure I want to have my life planted in the best soil that will reap an abundant harvest? Do I really want to go to the other side and see what God wants me to do for the kingdom in Jesus's name? As we grow closer to God in prayer, our answer will always be a resounding *yes* because serving God is the most fulfilling thing we will ever do! God will never take you anywhere He has not equipped you, just like He was equipping His disciples on that extraordinary day.

Jesus's heart's desire is always to do the will of the Father. He told His disciples, "*I seek not my own will but the will of him who sent me*" (John 5:30). The trip across the lake was a targeted activity for Him to accomplish the Father's will. I believe that in His spirit, Jesus heard the demon-possessed man's desperate cry from the other side of the lake. The lesson about the soil was designed so the disciples would understand the truth: if you really want to get in the boat with Jesus, your life will be about bringing God's love to those who are *the neediest*.

The violent storm was a designed spiritual attack from the enemy to get the boat off course so they would miss the landing spot where this man was in captivity.

Jesus demonstrated to His disciples that the violent storm on the Sea of Galilee was not a coincidence. It was not just a random storm. It was a designed spiritual attack from the enemy to get the boat off course so they would miss the landing spot where this man was in captivity. As an amateur boat captain, I can assure you that if your instruments are only 5 degrees off, you will not go where you want to go. You could miss the land completely. Showing up at this precise spot on the other side of the shore was due to the *heavenly minded GPS* inside of Jesus.

That day, Jesus was demonstrating that you can expect storms in life, especially when you believe you have God's direction to accomplish something for His kingdom. Don't quit! These storms are just trying to derail you from embracing the most exciting life possible.

Right now, let's go to the throne room together and pray that our understanding of God's purposes would be revealed to our hearts.

Please join us for prayer on Day 9 at:

www.acts413.net/deeperprayer
OR
www.strategicrenewal.com/21days-deeper-prayer

What About You, Storm Chaser?

Jim Maxim

For the Son of Man came to seek and to save the lost.
—Luke 19:10

Jesus stepped into the boat that day on the Sea of Galilee knowing there was a storm just ahead. *"And a great windstorm arose, and the waves were breaking into the boat, so that the boat was already filling"* (Mark 4:37). Reading the events from the fourth chapter of Mark, the Lord impressed upon me that Jesus was what I like to call a *storm chaser*. That's someone who is willing to face the storms in any situation in order to get to the other side and follow God's plan. A storm chaser surrenders to God's will and is excited to get in the boat with Jesus to see what's on the other side, even if storms lie ahead.

Through Jesus's example in the gospel of Mark, we just saw how a storm chaser uses the seed of God's Word to totally transform a life! *"For the Son of man came to seek and to save the lost"* (Luke 19:10). Everything that happened during Jesus's extraordinary day came about because *a lost soul was crying out to God for help*, and God sent His only Son personally to heal him and set him free from all that hell could throw at him. Now the disciples understood the reason Jesus wanted them to go over to the other side in the first place. They understood that if they were going to hang around with Jesus, they had better get used to rocky waves, dark clouds, and fearful moments in order to come to the rescue of people who need the love and redemption of God.

In His spirit, Jesus had heard this man's cry from the other side of the lake and even though a storm was brewing, Jesus would not be denied. He had an agenda for the disciples to see God's love and Word in action; He had a plan for this man, the demoniac, to be set free and healed. This lost man was marked for God's purposes from the beginning of time to become a son of the Most High God! (See Mark 5:18–20.)

> *God had ordained this trip across the lake to show the world that nobody is beyond the reach of His love.*

God had ordained this trip across the lake to show the world that nobody is beyond the reach of His love. Jesus wanted to teach the disciples and the church that the kingdom of God could be manifested right before our very eyes, that God did send *"His only begotten Son, that whoever believes in Him should not perish but have everlasting life"* (John 3:16 NKJV) and live with Him forever and ever. Jesus wanted to teach the disciples that they were chosen—just like you and me—to become storm chasers to extend the hand of God's love to everyone He brings into our lives.

Jesus calls us to become His agents on earth to dispense His love to those around us. He wants to flow through us in such a way that others realize that God's reservoir of love is always completely full. He reminds us that whatever need we are facing, Jesus Christ has the provision to meet it. Jesus longs for us to get in the boat with Him and has promised us that *"with God nothing will be impossible"* (Luke 1:37 NKJV).

God will still gently push me today, saying, "Come on, Jim, get in the boat and let's go over to the other side," even though I don't know exactly what awaits me. He reminds me that it is time to take the step of faith and just get in the boat and begin moving in the direction of what I sense He is saying in my heart, even if I don't understand it completely.

Jesus takes great pleasure when He sees us taking a step of faith in His name towards a storm we see in someone else's life. He knows that once we get out and take that step of faith into uncharted waters, fear, doubt, and unbelief are going to meet us. I am convinced that He is like the parent who tells a child to jump into the swimming pool because the child will certainly be caught. Jesus gets excited when we will stare fear right in the face and jump anyway.

> *For God has not given us a spirit of fear, but of power and of love and of a sound mind.* (2 Timothy 1:7 NKJV)

> *Have I not commanded you? Be strong and courageous. Do not be frightened, and do not be dismayed, for the LORD your God is with you wherever you go.* (Joshua 1:9)

There are storms that come up very fast on the water and we shouldn't be surprised how big and nasty they can get! But when you're following the leading of the Holy Spirit, Jesus inside of you has all the power in the universe to speak to the storms and command them to be still. God Almighty wants you to trust Him and allow Him to equip you with the faith and power that are necessary to calm the storms in your life and in the lives around you.

> *Be strong and courageous. Do not fear or be in dread of them, for it is the LORD your God who goes with you. He will not leave you or forsake you.* (Deuteronomy 31:6)

Jesus knows the fear we are feeling and the thoughts of insecurity and lack of ability we are fighting against. That's the reason it's called faith in the first place! Hebrews 11:1 (KJV) says, *"Now faith is the substance of things hoped for, the evidence of things not seen."* Faith is the actual evidence we have within us; we just can't see it with our natural eyes. We have to use the eyes of faith that Jesus gave us when He picked us up in our sin and washed us off with the blood He shed on Calvary. That's one of the reasons He sacrificed for us in the first place.

Remember, the storms we face are the fertilizers that activate the seed in us. When our hearts are filled with fear, doubt, and unbelief, that's the exact time God is just standing there cheering us on as our Father, saying, "Come on, this is the moment that I have designed for you! *You can do it because I said you can,* and I have placed within you the seed of heaven that thrives in this type of weather!"

Jesus always knows what storms are coming, and He would never allow them to come into our lives without first giving us the power to overcome them. We need to understand that *becoming a storm chaser* is really our first calling—because when we overcome those storms, we realize how much God loves us.

What about you, storm chaser? You have been handpicked by God; He has placed the supernatural seed of His Word in you and given you the *good soil* to receive it *so that you can go into a lost and dying world* and demonstrate the power of the gospel in very practical ways to everyone God places in your path.

You have received the privilege of giving away the unending reservoir of God's love that He deposited in you the day you asked Jesus to cleanse you and forgive you. Even though you didn't know that Jesus would say to you, *"Let us go across to the other side"* (Mark 4:35), this was His plan all along for you and all those who call themselves Christians. You are a storm chaser because the hurt and lost in this world need you.

Remember the description that the mob gave to those early disciples, *"These men who have turned the world upside down"* (Acts 17:6)? Those disciples had become storm chasers...will you? Will you get in the boat with Jesus and take the risk of becoming a storm chaser for His eternal glory?

Today we will pray to the God and Father who calls us to rescue those who are in need even through the storm.

Join us for prayer on Day 10 at:

www.acts413.net/deeperprayer
OR
www.strategicrenewal.com/21days-deeper-prayer

Wisdom Will Come into Your Heart

Jim Maxim

*He who gets wisdom loves his own soul; he who keeps
understanding will find good.*
—Proverbs 19:8 (NKJV)

*Wisdom is the principal thing; therefore get wisdom. And in all
your getting, get understanding.*
—Proverbs 4:7 (NKJV)

*I wisdom dwell with prudence,
and find out knowledge of witty inventions.*
—Proverbs 8:12 (KJV)

I have three sons, three daughters-in-law, three incredible grand-children, and my loving, sweet, good-looking wife, Cathy! As of this writing, I'm sixty-seven years old. I tell my kids my number is 132... and of course, they ask, "What's that, Dad?" My research shows that a man in Pennsylvania lives to an average age of seventy-eight. So, if I'm in the average, I have 132 months left to serve the Lord on this earth!

God could give me 240 months if He wanted to, of course, and I'll serve Him as long as I can, but my average would be 132.

What's my point here? *If I had one last message to give to my wife, my kids, or my grandkids, it's the message in this prayer day.* Why? Because *God's wisdom* is vital in our lives.

If you want to know how to become the person God has truly intended for you to be for His eternal glory, you need to understand what His Word says on the critical importance of wisdom. My favorite wisdom passage of all is Proverbs 2:1–12. Here God gives us twelve stepping-stones on the path to the supernatural wisdom that He wants us to walk in:

1. *My son, **if** you **receive** my words and **treasure up** my commandments with you,*

2. *Making your ear **attentive** to wisdom and **inclining your heart** to understanding;*

3. *Yes, if you **call out** for insight and **raise your voice** for understanding,*

4. *If you **seek** it like silver and **search** for it as for hidden treasures,*

5. *Then you will understand the fear of the LORD and **find the knowledge of God**.*

6. *For the LORD **gives wisdom**; from his mouth come knowledge and understanding;*

7. *He **stores up** sound wisdom for the upright; he is a **shield** to those who walk in integrity,*

8. *Guarding the paths of justice and **watching over** the way of his saints.*

9. *Then you will **understand** righteousness and justice and equity, every good path;*

10. *For **wisdom will come into your heart**, and knowledge will be pleasant to **your soul**;*

11. *Discretion will watch over you, understanding will **guard you**,*

12. ***Delivering you** from the way of evil, from men of perverted speech.*

Read those verses again. God is declaring to you and me that if we truly *listen* and *receive* the wisdom of His Word, if we *call out* to Him and *seek His wisdom* as if searching for treasure, then He will fill us with the wisdom that He has stored up for us, His children. Read verse 10 closely: *"For wisdom will come into your heart, and knowledge will be pleasant to your soul."* What a powerful promise from the God of the universe! The supernatural *wisdom, knowledge,* and *understanding* of God Almighty is available to *come into your heart and soul!*

> *The supernatural wisdom, knowledge, and understanding of God Almighty is available to come into your heart and soul!*

One more time: where will God's wisdom, knowledge, and understanding go? Into your heart and soul! Some people think these words can be interchanged with *mind*, but in this context, it's a much deeper meaning. The words *heart and soul* paint an eternal picture of what God is trying to tell us, that His wisdom will enter the depths of your being today, just like it would in Solomon's day when the Proverbs were written. In our lives today, these verses mean that God's perfect wisdom is available to you in every area if you will seek and receive it—wisdom for your marriage, your parenting, your ministry, your finances, your career, your relationships with family and friends, and on and on.

God is declaring in His Word that if you follow these instructions, placing Him and His Word first in your life, then His hand of blessing will rest upon you and everything you do. If you follow His instructions, wisdom will guide your mind and heart to keep you focused on just *why* He wants you to have these blessings in your life. That *why* holds an important truth. God wants you to be what He has intended all along for His eternal glory, which is the person you really want to be deep in your heart. The wisdom, knowledge, and understanding you receive from God and His Word will reveal to you how that is possible.

> *I wisdom dwell with prudence, and find out knowledge of witty inventions.*
> (Proverbs 8:12 KJV)

This is another wisdom verse that has meant a lot to me personally. "*Witty inventions*" are new, exciting ideas, and fresh plans revealed to us through the wisdom of God. I'm a business owner, so for me, this verse means asking God for His wisdom and witty inventions in how to run my business, to show me "*great and hidden things that* [I] *have not known*" (Jeremiah 33:3) in a way that would be successful and bring Him honor. God has been so faithful to answer me in ways that I would never have imagined.

The prophet Joshua reminds us of the importance of God's Word:

> *This Book of the Law shall not depart from your mouth, but you shall mediate on it day and night, **so that** you may be careful to do according to all that is written in it. For then you will make your way prosperous, and then you will have good success.*
> (Joshua 1:8)

Let's go to the throne room and pray for the understanding of how to walk in the wisdom and knowledge of these verses in God's Word.

Join us for prayer on Day 11 at:

www.acts413.net/deeperprayer
OR
www.strategicrenewal.com/21days-deeper-prayer

Don't Feel Like Praying?

Eph 6:
16 +8
verses ?

Daniel Henderson

Over the years, I have been amazed at the paltry desire I've felt to pray. I am especially aware of this aversion just prior to the times that I've specifically set aside to pray, whether in private or with others. I suppose this confession may come as a surprise. Yet, I hope you are comforted by the admission that you are not alone in your weak longings when the hour of prayer arrives.

I see four reasons for this lack of motivation:

1. THE INDEPENDENCE OF THE FLESH

I have said many times that prayerlessness is our declaration of independence from God. I heard one teacher describe us as "spirit critters in an earth suit." Our new man desires God, but our flesh wants to live independently. In the natural, we resist humble reliance on God and transparent intimacy with other believers, both of which are germane to real prayer.

When we feel apathy toward prayer, we need to recognize the prayer-oriented desires of the Spirit in our hearts and give them priority over the resistance of our flesh, which tends toward self-reliance, self-protection, and self-determination.

2. THE RELENTLESS ATTACK OF THE ENEMY

I've heard it said, "No one is a firmer believer in the power of prayer than the devil; not that he practices it, but he suffers from it."

Pastor Jim Cymbala has noted, "The devil is not terribly frightened of our human efforts and credentials. But he knows his kingdom will be damaged when we begin to lift up our hearts to God."

Satan and his demons seek to counter and diminish every intention of the Christian toward prayer. We need to recognize the role that prayer plays in the spiritual battle (see Ephesians 6:16–18) and resolve to be *praying menaces* to the enemy of our souls.

3. THE BUSYNESS OF OUR MODERN LIVES

Busyness destroys relationships, starting with our primary relationship, the one we have with God. I am convinced that busyness is the breeding ground of self-sufficiency and lures us into the deceptive life pattern that concludes that we can conduct our Christian life by our own efforts rather than through a humble and heartfelt abiding in Christ through prayer. I am reminded of the familiar adage that if the devil cannot make us bad, he will simply keep us busy.

Charles Spurgeon wrote, "Sometimes we think we are too busy to pray. That also is a great mistake, for praying is a saving of time.… If we have no time we must make time, for if God has given us time for secondary duties, he must have given us time for primary ones, and to draw near to him is a primary duty, and we must let nothing set it on one side."[2]

---

2. "Pray Without Ceasing," Charles Haddon Spurgeon, March 10, 1872, from *Metropolitan Tabernacle Pulpit Vol. 18*, The Spurgeon Center (www.spurgeon.org/resource-library/sermons/pray-without-ceasing).

4. THE UNPLEASANT MEMORY OF PREVIOUS EXPERIENCES

Dave Butts, author and chairman of America's National Prayer Committee, often states that "the main reason most people do not attend prayer meetings at their church is because they have been to prayer meetings at their church."

Sadly, many people give in to their excuses about prayer because their past experiences have been traditional rather than biblical, man-centered rather than God-centered, and request-based rather than worship-based. Few Christians really enjoy this unfortunate dilution and diversion from real New Testament prayer.

Now, from my own journey in personal and corporate prayer, I see *four vital ingredients* for breaking through our reluctance in prayer to enjoy the Lord's gift of intimacy with Him.

1. MIND YOUR MOTIVATION

Like the Pharisees Jesus called out in Matthew 6:5, we can be motivated by improper pursuits. For them, it was praying for *show*, to be seen by others. For us, it could be guilt, duty, or even a resolve to manipulate God into doing our will on earth rather than His. Because God convicted me early in my ministry about my need to become a praying pastor who led a praying church, I committed to personally holding multiple prayer gatherings every week with my congregation. After well over two decades of this rhythm, God privileged me to participate with my people in thousands of prayer experiences. But here is a confession: I did not *feel* like going to most of those gatherings.

*The only enduring motivation for prayer is that
God is worthy to be sought.*

Why did I still pursue these prayer meetings? Early in the journey, the Lord emblazoned a motivation into my heart that consistently overcame my excuses and reluctance. I focused on the truth that the only enduring motivation for prayer is that God is worthy to be sought. This paramount reality never changes. This worship-based focus fueled consistent resolve and genuine desire. It transformed my prayer life and how our church prayed. When enthusiasm wanes and the enemy strikes, I say it aloud: "God is worthy to be sought! I will choose to pray!"

2. PLACE ACTION ABOVE FEELING

Real prayer, like other important issues in life, cannot be mastered by feeling our way into action, but rather by acting our way into feeling. Prayer is not a mood. Prayer is the lifeline of all that is good and must be chosen in spite of current feelings, impulses, and conveniences. The more we understand God's worthiness, the more we grasp our neediness and the deeper our conviction takes root. We must pray, regardless of circumstances or spiritually counterproductive urges.

3. AVOID A FALSE START

On the walls of my childhood home hung a plaque that read, "When it seems hardest to pray, pray hardest." I would revise that to say, "When it seems hardest to pray, worship passionately." Too many times, our starting place in prayer is simply the articulation of whatever is on our minds to say to God. Let's be honest: our human thoughts are often misguided, shallow, and punctuated as the beginning place of prayer. This is usually a false start.

That is why I have concluded that the best beginning point in prayer is from the pages of God's Word. His truth gives our hearts language, especially as it provides truth and fresh insight about His character, His names, and His mighty works. God's Word quickly sparks a new motivation for prayer, regardless of our mood or circumstances, by fixing our eyes on Him and opening our hearts to His Word to us, not just our words to Him.

4. BE COMPELLED BY COMMUNITY

The Lord never designed us to learn prayer on a discouraging solo journey. He has placed us in a body so that our worship, learning, fellowship, and prayers might be powerfully enjoyed in community. All of the New Testament commands to pray were written to believers in community and applied instinctively in corporate prayer, since there were no personal or individualized copies of Scripture until the advent of the printing press.

Teaching on the model prayer Jesus laid out in the New Testament, noted author and seminary president Albert Mohler wrote:

> Do you notice what is stunningly absent? There is no first-person singular pronoun in the entire prayer.... One of the besetting sins of evangelicalism is our obsession with individualism.... The first-person singular pronoun reigns in our thinking. We tend to think about nearly everything (including the truths of God's Word) only as they relate to *me*. This is why, when Jesus teaches his disciples to pray, he emphasizes from the very outset that we are part of a corporate people called the church. God is not merely "my Father." He is "our Father"—the Father of my brothers and

sisters in the faith with whom I identify and with whom I pray.[3]

When we pray together, motivation soars through the encouragement, accountability, and edification of the Spirit working through others to inspire our hearts. Of course, the very commitment to show up and pray with others keeps us regular in prayer. Alternatively, going it alone is the impetus for easy excuses and neglect of prayer.

Prayer is often our last resort rather than our first resolve. Yet, the more we learn about why our motivation wanes and how we can find consistent inspiration, the more faithful and fruitful we can be as we seek Him and grow in our Christlikeness through prayer.

With this motivation in mind, let's pray together now.

Join us for prayer on Day 12 at:

www.acts413.net/deeperprayer
OR
www.strategicrenewal.com/21days-deeper-prayer

---

3. R. Albert Mohler, Jr., "The Danger of 'I' in Christian Prayer," Aug. 20, 2018 (albertmohler.com/2018/08/20/danger-christian-prayer).

Seeking God When Life
Is Uncertain

Daniel Henderson

*Trust in him at all times, O people; pour out your heart before
him; God is a refuge for us.*
—Psalm 62:8

Prayer is the most tangible expression of trust in God.
—*Jerry Bridges*

I used to say that we live in uncertain times. While I still believe this is true, I am starting to conclude that we all live uncertain lives. While God's truth and our eternal destiny in Christ are certain, many other factors in our journey are quite unpredictable and unclear. It is the nature of the battle.

I suppose today, as you read this, you face some measure of uncertainty. You may face major questions about your health, your job, your finances, your children, your grandchildren, your church, or someone in your circle of friends. Clearly, we cannot avoid uncertainty in this life, but we can respond to it in a Christ-honoring and soul-profiting fashion.

THE SEARCH FOR CLARITY

I recently read a profound interchange between the renowned ethicist John Kavanaugh and Mother Teresa. He tells of a time in his life when he went to Calcutta to work for three months at "the house of the dying." This experience was part of his heartfelt search for direction about his future. His first morning there, Mother Teresa asked, "And what can I do for you?" Kavanaugh asked her to pray for him.

"What do you want me to pray for?" she asked. He explained that he had come thousands of miles from the U.S. to find direction and asked her to "pray that I have clarity." She said firmly, "No, I will not do that.… Clarity is the last thing you are clinging to and must let go of."

Kavanaugh commented that she always seemed to have the clarity he longed for.

She laughed. "I have never had clarity," she said. "What I have always had is trust. So I will pray that you trust God."

CLARITY VS. TRUST

There is something in all of us that wants clarity. It is part of our sinful ego and a common expression of our insecurities. Clarity can become an idol that replaces authentic trust in God. In many ways, we would rather understand the details of the road ahead than rest in deep intimacy with the God who has promised to direct our steps.

God has never promised to show us a detailed ten-year plan. Clarity can actually become spiritually counterproductive as it short-changes trust, a life of prayer, and moment-by-moment dependence on God. Certainty can actually breed complacency in our passionate pursuit of the heart and mind of God.

Scripture tells us, *"Trust in him at all times, O people; pour out your heart before him; God is a refuge for us"* (Psalm 62:8). Yes, we must pour out our hearts and all they contain, including praise and gratitude as well as worry, fear, doubt, and uncertainty. God is our in-the-moment refuge, but not always a divine GPS system, announcing the details of every turn we might encounter one year down the road. Thus, we must open our hearts wide in prayer and trust Him at *all* times. We should never assume a life of trust or take God's refuge for granted.

In the Epistles' great *faith* chapter, Hebrews 11, we are reminded that trust is strongest when clarity is dim or nonexistent. Noah built an ark while waiting for 120 years for an unprecedented rainfall. Sarah was told to trust God for a child in her old age with no clarity about how such a thing could happen. Abraham *"went out, not knowing where he was going"* (verse 8) and later planned to sacrifice his own son with no clarity about why he was called to do this or what the outcome might be. The stories are extensive. The truth is unmistakable. Faith flourishes when we are trusting God at the deepest level, with a willingness to let go of our insistence on clarity.

We often want to *chart the course*, but the Bible tells us to walk in the Spirit. We insist on a strategic plan, but Jesus says, "Follow Me." We want *all the answers*, but the Lord tells us to trust Him because of what we know to be true about His character. He calls us to an intimate knowledge of Himself as our confidence and security.

FAITH TO SEEK AND PLEASE GOD

Friend, as you go through uncertain days, realize the gift you've been given. The prayer of faith, not certainty, is the single most important ingredient to a life pleasing to God. (See Hebrews 11:6.)

Do you feel like you are in a fog today? Have you been there far too long? Does the present moment feel shaky while the future is unclear?

Remember, God is a rewarder of those who diligently seek *Him*, usually without clarity about the details. Looking back, we see His faithfulness and goodness, even if we did not perceive it at the time. He has not changed. You can trust Him now, even though His way seems ambiguous. Prayer is trust on its knees.

A few years ago, I discovered a song by a Christian musician named Jadon Lavik. The lyrics offer deep encouragement:

> *You wake up to find that you're right where you're supposed to be—trapped in uncertainty. Each day's a mystery. You wake up to find that you're right where you're supposed to be. The past is unveiled and you see you're right where you're meant to be.*[4]

We've heard it said often, but must live it obediently: when we can't trace His hand, we can trust His heart. I pray our hearts will likewise search less for clarity and more for the character of God as we draw near to Him in the unpredictable seasons of our journey. Join me now as we express our trust in our God who never fails.

Join us for prayer on Day 13 at:

www.acts413.net/deeperprayer
OR
www.strategicrenewal.com/21days-deeper-prayer

---

4. Jadon Lavik, "Meant to Be," on *Life on the Inside* (BEC Recordings, 2006).

Day 14

How the Holy Spirit Ignites Our Prayers[5]

Daniel Henderson

But you, beloved, building yourselves up in your most holy faith and praying in the Holy Spirit.
—Jude 1:20

A few years ago, my wife Rosemary and I spoke at a women's gathering on a Saturday morning. After the breakfast, a mother and daughter from the church gave the first presentation. We were scheduled to follow them on the program.

Their story was riveting.

Linda Barrick and her daughter, Jen, gave an account of the events that took place on a Sunday evening, November 5, 2006. As the family drove home from church, a drunk driver traveling 80 miles per hour struck their minivan head-on. Linda and her husband, Andy, were in the front. Fifteen-year-old Jen and eleven-year-old Josh were in the back. All sustained life-threatening injuries and were rushed to emergency rooms at different hospitals.

5. This chapter is adapted from Daniel Henderson's book *Transforming Prayer: How Everything Changes When You Seek God's Face* (Minneapolis, MN: Bethany House Publishers, 2011).

While all four family members were in serious condition, doctors did not expect Jen to live through the night. But God sustained her life. She remained in a coma for five weeks with traumatic brain injuries and multiple skull fractures. Jen's slow emergence from the coma took many more weeks. Doctors feared the brain injuries might prompt a flurry of strange behaviors, such as screaming or cursing. Instead, Jen's spirit poured out with praise songs and constant prayers. Even though she was not cognizant of her injuries, her location, or even the names of her family members, she continued to praise God.

"The Holy Spirit was so alive and evident in her," her mom commented.

Unable to open her eyes or comprehend her surroundings, Jen literally prayed for hours.

"But she did not ask for one thing," recounts Linda. "Even with her body thrashing back and forth uncontrollably, she would cry out for hours, 'Lord, you are so good. Lord, you are so faithful.'"

Linda notes, "I would just sit there and weep as the Spirit enabled her to praise her Father, sing worship songs, and even quote Scriptures. It was as if she had been in His presence the whole time."[6]

THE REALM OF THE HOLY SPIRIT

Today, Jen has recovered remarkably well, but still suffers memory loss and endures cortical blindness. Yet she is able and eager to join her mother regularly in telling this amazing account of God's grace and the power of prayer. As Rosemary and I listened to the Barricks' story, we were struck by this truth: the Holy Spirit produces truth-based worship and thanksgiving in the hearts of His children.

6. For information about the Barricks' story, including testimonies and videos, visit hopeoutloud.com.

The Holy Spirit produces truth-based worship and thanksgiving in the hearts of His children.

Beyond our mental and physical capacities exists a spiritual dimension that we must grasp if we are going to learn to pray by the power of the Holy Spirit. Worship-based prayer brings our hearts into intimate harmony with the person of the Holy Spirit and enhances our surrender to His control, wisdom, and power for our prayers. The Spirit then enables us to worship more deeply. This worship, in turn, brings us a greater surrender to the Spirit, thus continuing the circle.

Jen Barrick, with limited mental and physical capacity, exhibited a profound experience of prayer in the realm of the Holy Spirit. Many of us depend on our own intellect and forget the Holy Spirit's essential role. We may punch the prayer clock, but transformation eludes us.

GRAVEYARD OR INSANE ASYLUM

My friend Jim Cymbala urges Christians toward a vibrant, practical, and balanced reliance on the Holy Spirit. He notes that when it comes to the person of the Holy Spirit, churches tend to be either cemeteries or insane asylums. Some hardly recognize the Holy Spirit or seek Him at all. Others engage in all kinds of bizarre, extra-biblical antics, for which the Holy Spirit gets "credit." In our prayers, we want to avoid these extremes, but must set our hearts on the very real, powerful, and practical reality of the Holy Spirit.

LIVING AND PRAYING IN THE SPIRIT

In his book *Forgotten God*, Francis Chan writes:

From my perspective, the Holy Spirit is tragically neglected and, for all practical purposes, forgotten. While no evangelical would deny His existence, I'm willing to bet there are millions of churchgoers across America who cannot confidently say they have experienced His presence or action in their lives over the past year. And many of them do not believe they can.[7]

Chan continues:

If I were Satan and my ultimate goal was to thwart God's kingdom and purposes, one of my main strategies would be to get churchgoers to ignore the Holy Spirit…but when believers live in the power of the Spirit, the evidence in their lives is supernatural. The church cannot help but be different, and the world cannot help but notice.[8]

Jesus wants His house and His people to be characterized by prayer. (See Mark 11:17.) The Lord wants us to be controlled and empowered by the supernatural reality of His Holy Spirit rather than by human strategies and intellectual prowess.

THE HOLY SPIRIT AND THE "HOW TO"

I often ponder why the early church prayed like they did and we, in modern society, don't do so. The answer, I have concluded, is that they actually believed that the Holy Spirit *was* the "how to" of the Christian life.

We tend to think the Holy Spirit *helps us* in the Christian life. We treat Him like an app on our phone in our living and praying when, in reality, He is the operating system of our faith. Too often, the Holy Spirit is an afterthought rather than the first thought in our prayers.

7. Francis Chan, *Forgotten God* (Colorado Springs, CO: David C. Cook, 2009), 15.
8. Ibid., 16.

Without Him, no believer can pray effectively. Even the great apostle Paul confessed this truth about his own prayers. (See Romans 8:26.)

We are commanded to pray in the Spirit. (See Jude 1:20.) Greek scholar Kenneth Wuest explained, "Praying in the Spirit is praying in dependence on the Holy Spirit. It is prayer exercised in the sphere of the Holy Spirit, motivated and empowered by Him."[9]

Pastor John Piper defines it simply: "Praying in the Holy Spirit is to be moved and guided by the Holy Spirit in prayer. We pray by His power and according to His direction."[10]

The great Puritan writer William Law explained:

Read whatever chapter of scripture you will and be ever so delighted with it—yet it will leave you as poor, as empty and unchanged as it found you unless it has turned you wholly and solely to the Spirit of God, and brought you into full union with and dependence on Him.[11]

J. Oswald Sanders wrote, "Prayer in the Spirit is prayer whose supreme object is the glory of God, and only in a secondary sense is it a blessing for ourselves or for others."[12]

The Holy Spirit is the secret to Christ-honoring, deeper, and transforming prayer. This, I believe, is what Jen Barrick experienced during her slow recovery in a hospital bed. And it is what God desires for us in our prayer lives.

9. Kenneth S. Wuest, *Ephesians and Colossians in the Greek New Testament* (Grand Rapids, MI: Eerdmans, 1953), 145.
10. John Piper sermon, "Learning to Pray in the Spirit and the Word," Part 2, Jan. 7, 2001 (www.desiringgod.org).
11. William Law, *The Power of the Spirit* (Fort Washington, PA: Christian Literature Crusade, 1971), 19.
12. J. Oswald Sanders, *Prayer Power Unlimited* (Chicago, IL: Moody Press, 1977), 62.

So, now recognizing and relying on the Holy Spirit, let's pray together on Day 14 at:

www.acts413.net/deeperprayer
OR
www.strategicrenewal.com/21days-deeper-prayer

Day 15

Learn to Wrestle Well

Jim Maxim

> For **we do not wrestle against flesh and blood**, but against the
> rulers, against the authorities, against the cosmic powers over
> this present darkness, against the spiritual forces of evil in the
> heavenly places.
> —Ephesians 6:12

Have you ever considered what could be hindering you from your breakthrough personally, physically, mentally, emotionally, or financially? Could it be that you are wrestling with the wrong opponent in your life? The word *wrestle* means to take part in a fight, either as sport or in earnest, by grappling with one's opponent and trying to throw or force them to the ground.

As Christians, we aren't supposed to wrestle with other people no matter how much we think they're the problem. We are called to wrestle against *spiritual forces*:

+ *Against the rulers*

+ *Against the authorities*

+ *Against the cosmic powers*

+ *Against the spiritual forces of evil in the heavenly places*

I am emphasizing the real spiritual battle we are in because Jesus and His disciples had so much to say about our real enemy. They gave us strong warning. Don't be ignorant! Don't ignore it!

> *That we would not be outwitted by Satan; for **we are not ignorant of his designs.*** (2 Corinthians 2:11)

> ***Be sober-minded; be watchful.*** *Your adversary the devil prowls around like a roaring lion, seeking someone to devour. Resist him, firm in the faith.* (1 Peter 5:8–9)

> *Finally, be strong in the Lord and in the strength of his might. Put on the whole armor of God, that you may be able to stand **against the schemes of the devil.*** (Ephesians 6:10–11)

Why does the Bible have so much to say about our spiritual adversary? Because this warfare between Satan and the human race began a long time ago in the garden of Eden. I believe this spiritual warfare exists because Satan hates us; he is jealous of believers in Christ. Simply put, he will never again be able to receive God's love. He will never be reinstated to the position he once had before almighty God.

> *You were an anointed guardian cherub. I placed you; you were on the holy mountain of God…till unrighteousness was found in you.* (Ezekiel 28:14–15)

Satan can never be forgiven and permitted to sense God's holy presence. He is jealous of us and wants to steal or destroy any good thing God has given to us. Jesus declared, "*The thief* [Satan] *comes only to steal and kill and destroy. I came that they* [all believers] *may have life and have life abundantly*" (John 10:10).

Jesus also told us that we should *"be wise as serpents and as gentle as doves"* (Matthew 10:16). We are not wise but foolish if we don't train ourselves and others to understand exactly what is fighting against us. Paul went to great lengths to educate the body of Christ about successfully living for Jesus and being a soldier of His kingdom against the real enemy. Paul wrote, *"We wanted to come to you—even I, Paul, time and again—but Satan hindered us"* (1 Thessalonians 2:18 NKJV). If Satan could hinder the apostle Paul, don't you think he could hinder *you?*

Please don't think I'm saying these spiritual forces can force you to do anything; they cannot. My desire is to give you the facts about who you are in the eyes of God and why you need the authority He has given you. You are God's child, and He wants you to have *"rivers of living water"* flowing from your innermost being (see John 7:38), but our spiritual enemy wants to do what he can to hinder you in your walk, to keep you from reaching God's divine purpose for your life. That is why the Bible tells us to *be watchful* and *resist the devil.* Being properly equipped is the key to success in anything. In the spiritual world, it's not how much money you have, or what schools you attended, or any of the natural things we generally look at to determine success. It's the power of God's Word.

> For though we walk in the flesh, we are not waging war according to the flesh. For the weapons of our warfare are not of the flesh but have divine power to destroy strongholds. We destroy arguments and every lofty opinion raised against the knowledge of God, and take every thought captive to obey Christ.
>
> (2 Corinthians 10:3–5)

As believers, we don't have to live in fear of the supernatural. God has given us powerful weapons against temptation and accusation. He has given us weapons of warfare, prayer, the Word, and our faith to stand strong and resist. *"But the Lord is faithful, and he will strengthen you and protect you from the evil one"* (2 Thessalonians 3:3 NIV).

Thank God for Jesus Christ, who gave His life to deliver us from the hands of the enemy.

> *But you are a chosen race, a royal priesthood, a holy nation, a people for his own possession, that you may proclaim the excellencies of him **who called you out of darkness** into his marvelous light.* (1 Peter 2:9)

> *He has **delivered us from the domain of darkness** and transferred us to the kingdom of his beloved Son.* (Colossians 1:13)

Wow, almighty God loves you! He loves you, He loves you, He loves you! You are redeemed. He has taken you from the kingdom of darkness into His marvelous light!

Now, I know that spiritual warfare can sound weird to some people. I know if you have this conversation with someone who is not walking with God, they can look at you like you're uneducated or crazy. It's happened to me plenty of times! But the apostle Paul had that problem covered 2,000 years ago!

> *But people who aren't spiritual **can't receive** these truths from God's Spirit. It all sounds foolish to them and they can't understand it, for only those who are spiritual can understand what the Spirit means.* (1 Corinthians 2:14 NLT)

To be ignorant of the facts about spiritual warfare doesn't make it any less true. And since God's Word tells us that it *is* true, don't you want to win this wrestling match?

Let's go to the throne of God in prayer together today and battle for those who are being hindered. We will take the shield of faith and quench all the darts of the wicked one coming against anyone God has placed on your heart!

Join us for prayer on Day 15 at:

www.acts413.net/deeperprayer
OR
www.strategicrenewal.com/21days-deeper-prayer

Jonathan
Hannah
Mary Rogers

From Darkness to Light

Jim Maxim

*He has delivered us from the domain of darkness and
transferred us to the kingdom of his beloved Son.*
—Colossians 1:13

I'm going to make a strong statement here that might surprise you. When I met Jesus Christ, He radically stopped Satan from killing me. He demonstrated His power over the enemy to completely destroy the stranglehold he had on my life. He forced Satan to release me from the chains he had linked around my soul. Psalm 107:14–15 (NKJV) says, "[God] *brought them out of darkness and the shadow of death, and broke their chains in pieces. Oh, that men would give thanks to the LORD for His goodness, and for His wonderful works to the children of men!*" That is what God Almighty did for me.

God rescued me because one godly woman cried out to Him with faith in His love, His power, and His commitment to answer the prayers of His people. This woman was my mother, Isobel, and she had a God in heaven who we knew actually listened to her. She prayed with such openness and expectancy as if He were her closest friend! She would take spiritual authority over fear, doubt, and unbelief, and just *bring her God and*

His power down upon us and into the situation. She looked past the natural into the supernatural and focused on the truth that God really is almighty and that He always has the final word about whatever happens in our life.

Isobel had a deeper understanding of the power of prayer than most Christians and understood how to battle in the spiritual realm. She learned that going into God's presence in daily prayer, and taking her prayer needs before the one and only Holy God, meant that all things were possible. *"But Jesus looked at them and said, 'With man this is impossible, but with God all things are possible'"* (Matthew 19:26). In prayer, by prayer, and through prayer, God has chosen to move on behalf of His people.

After Isobel prayed for me to be released from my rebellious life and the strongholds that had me bound, she praised God for hearing and answering her prayers before she even saw the answer. Many people think it isn't rational to praise God before we have answered prayer. But Isobel knew her God worked by faith, and that praise would pull down all of the negative thoughts attacking her mind about the ungodly life I was living. And God miraculously answered her prayers and praise and delivered me literally from death. The book *Face to Face with God*[13] is the testimony of my early life.

My mother's prayer and praise pulled down the strongholds that I had permitted Satan to have on me through my lifestyle and choices. *"For though we walk in the flesh, we are not waging war according to the flesh. For the weapons of our warfare are not of the flesh **but have divine power to destroy strongholds**"* (2 Corinthians 10:3–4). We must grasp this truth: we have the power in Jesus to destroy strongholds!

We must grasp this truth: we have the power in Jesus to destroy strongholds!

13. Jim Maxim, *Face-to-Face with God: A True Story of Rebellion and Restoration* (New Kensington, PA: Whitaker House, 2011).

What is a stronghold? In the natural, a stronghold is a place that has been fortified and strengthened, such as a fort. Spiritually, it is a thought, plan, or action with a hold on our lives that stands against the knowledge of God and His Word. Satan tries to fortify those negative thoughts or plans in our minds and use them to keep us in bondage and away from freedom in Christ. That's why we must recognize that Satan is a real enemy and not just someone's dark imagination.

Can you see why prayer is so important in the life of the church? When you recognize the power of prayer, can you see why Satan hates prayer? Can you see why he tries to make personal and corporate prayer so unattractive to Christians? When was the last time you or your church had a prayer meeting packed with people *pulling down strongholds* for the lost in their lives? *Ouch!* I'm not trying to throw guilt or condemnation on anyone. Daniel and I just want to see the church wake up. We want to equip you to grow in Christ, to become more productive for the kingdom of God, to be a spiritual warrior in prayer for your family, your friends, your pastor, your church, your career, your neighbors, the country, and the world. We want people to say of us what they said of the early Christians in Acts 17:6: *"These men who have turned the world upside down have come here also."*

Here are a few reasons why Satan tries to hinder Christian prayer:

1. The church was designed by God to only receive power from Him through prayer. Isaiah 40:31 (NKJV) says, *"But those who wait on the LORD shall renew their strength; they shall mount up with wings like eagles, they shall run and not be weary, they shall walk and not faint."*

2. Satan knows that true spiritual power, pulling down spiritual strongholds, only happens when we call upon God in prayer. So, he has gone to great lengths to fill our minds with every negative thought possible about how prayer is "not really accomplishing anything."

3.   Christians, leaders, and the average person sitting in the pew often have the misconception that *doing something* accomplishes more for God than first spending time saturating their efforts with prayer. The truth is, walking on prayed-over ground will permit our efforts to be much more effective. *"The effective prayer of a righteous man can accomplish much"* (James 5:16 NASB).

4.   Satan knows that prayer will stop his destructive plans. *"In all circumstances take up the shield of faith, with which you can extinguish all the flaming darts of the evil one; and take the helmet of salvation, and the sword of the Spirit, which is the word of God, **praying at all times in the Spirit, with all prayer and supplication**. To that end, keep alert with all perseverance"* (Ephesians 6:16–18).

What strongholds do you want to see destroyed in your life or the life of a loved one or a friend? *"We destroy every proud obstacle that keeps people from knowing God. We capture their rebellious thoughts and teach them to obey Christ"* (2 Corinthians 10:5 NLT). Who do you know with rebellious or negative thoughts that are destroying their minds, thoughts that are preventing them from knowing Jesus Christ as their personal Lord and Savior? I said earlier that I want to see you and those you love unshackled, unstuck, and unhindered. Satan can bind us up, but Jesus can set us free. *"So if the Son sets you free, you will be free indeed"* (John 8:36).

Let's pray together with the power of God's Word to free us and those we love. We will ask almighty God to break any strongholds that have bound us or those we know, praying that those who need Jesus will surrender themselves to God's love and the cross of Jesus Christ.

Join us for prayer on Day 16 at:

www.acts413.net/deeperprayer
OR
www.strategicrenewal.com/21days-deeper-prayer

Snatching Them Out of the Fire

Jim Maxim

Have mercy on those who doubt; **save others by snatching them
out of the fire;** *to others show mercy with fear, hating even the
garment stained by the flesh.*
—Jude 1:22–23

Have you ever snatched someone out of the fire? Have you thought
about it much at all? Please allow me to have a heart-to-heart talk with
you for a moment. Who comes to mind when you think about those
you love or know who do not know Jesus? I know the thought of them
being lost for eternity upsets you deeply, and yet most Christians don't
spend much time, if any, doing anything about it.

Please stay with me for just a few minutes. I promise you this
prayer day will not be a guilt trip heaped on you about soul winning.
It is meant to help you see just how much God longs for you to *engage
with Him daily* so that you can understand the area closest to His heart.

*For God so loved the world, that He gave His only begotten Son,
that whoever believes in Him shall not perish, but have eternal
life.* (John 3:16 NASB)

We can't save a soul by ourselves anyway; it's only done in the power of the Holy Spirit. Instead, as we grow deeper in our relationship with God Almighty, we recognize that He has a special place for each of us in reaching others for Jesus Christ. Even though it's not the same way for everyone, each one of us is just as important to Him.

> *You did not choose Me but I chose you, and **appointed you that you would go and bear fruit,** and that your fruit would remain.*
>
> (John 15:16 NASB)

In reaching the lost for Jesus, we are answering this call to bear fruit that remains. We don't have to be a famous evangelist like Billy Graham. In fact, most of us will never preach a sermon on Sunday morning, write a book, or even lead a Bible study. But there is a place for all of us to follow the Holy Spirit's appointed call to be a fruit-bearing Christian in this way. Of course, we bear fruit in other ways in our Christian life, but the one closest to God's heart is the reason He sent His Son into the world in the first place, so that *none would perish.* They would be snatched from the fire to enjoy eternal life with the Almighty.

Do you believe it takes gas to run your vehicle? Well, your belief doesn't do you any good unless you go to the pump and get gas! Perhaps you're low on fuel in your fruit-bearing spiritual activity because you have not been going to the right pump.

Maybe you're thinking, *Jim, I can't speak in front of a large group like you do.* But perhaps God is calling you to lead a smaller group or Bible study, or invite people who don't know Jesus to your home to open doors for the gospel.

Are you quiet or introverted? Is it hard for you to speak to strangers about the Lord? Maybe God is calling you to intercede for those who are dying without Him.

Do you understand the fruit you can actually bear in your prayers? You can snatch someone out of the fire through your intercession! God is waiting for all of us to ask to be used to share the gospel with the lost.

> *You can snatch someone out of the fire through your intercession! God is waiting for us to ask to be used to share the gospel with the lost.*

Prayer is the activity that allows us to engage with God every single day. That not only puts us in the position to receive from Him, but prayer can also accomplish great things for His purposes and for His glory. E. M. Bounds wrote, "The Gospel cannot live, fight, conquer without prayer— prayer unceasing, instant and ardent."

Can you imagine what a praying church could accomplish? How much more strength would our pastors, their wives, and their families receive if we cried out to God consistently every day for them? How many of our friends and loved ones would be saved and delivered if we cried out to God daily for them? How much more productive would our careers be if we cried out to God daily and asked for His almighty hand to move the obstacles in our path? If we asked Him for His wisdom about the situations we, or our children, were confronting? How much more would our country want to honor God if we consistently cried out to Him?

Saving others by snatching them out of the fire is crucial to a God who sent Jesus to seek and save the lost. Sadly, according to statistics on evangelism, 95 percent of all Christians have never won a soul to Christ. Nearly 49 percent of leadership ministries spend *no time* in an average week ministering outside of the church, and 89 percent of leadership ministries have *no time* for evangelism on their list of weekly priorities.

I believe that God has a place and plan for each of us, not just spiritual leaders, to reach the lost for Jesus, and He will use the specific gifts He has given you. What really matters is what God wants from me—what God wants from you—and receiving from Him the ability to do whatever that is. *Receiving from Him* is the key. When I humble myself in His presence, ask my heavenly Father to forgive me for anything in my life not pleasing to Him, fill me fresh daily with His presence, and give me His wisdom, knowledge, and understanding, I am now in the position to receive from Him whatever it is I need to fulfill my mission for His kingdom and His eternal glory. I can pray daily, "Father, please use me today to make faith come alive in someone's heart somewhere today."

Let's look at the fifteenth chapter of John again:

> *You did not choose me, but I chose you and appointed you so that you might go and bear fruit—fruit that will last—and so that whatever you ask in my name the Father will give you.*
>
> (John 15:16 NIV)

Whatever we ask the Father in the name of Jesus, He will give it to us! That is a promise from God that is clearly conditioned on us bearing the fruit that grows as we abide in Him. *"I am the vine; you are the branches. Whoever abides in me and I in him, he it is that bears much fruit, for apart from me you can do nothing"* (John 15:5). Only God can make the fruit grow; we cannot do it on our own. Our part is abiding in Him.

God has a promise for us attached to His appointment to bear fruit for Him. He didn't have to promise us anything, but He did. Now I can go confidently to my Father in prayer and ask Him for the things I am seeking from Him. I can now rest assured that if what I am asking from Him is in His will for me, I will receive it.

> *This is the confidence that we have toward him, that if we ask anything according to his will he hears us. And if we know that he*

hears us in whatever we ask, we know that we have the requests
that we have asked of him.

(1 John 5:14–15)

Since God has placed me in the business world, He wants me to be successful there, so many of my personal prayers over the years have been in that area. I still have to challenge my heart, "Am I really doing this for His glory or for mine?" If I stay before God daily in an attitude of humility and gratitude, and keep my focus first on His kingdom, I am in a position to receive the answered prayer and the blessing God would like to give to me as His son. When our first priorities are pleasing Him and doing those things that please Him, our selfish hearts more easily stay submitted to His will and not our own.

I want to please my heavenly Father and use the gifts He has given me. Since God has appointed us to bear fruit, let's accept from Him the ability to perform our part in His kingdom. Let's step into the appointment or position in His kingdom that He has ordained for us.

Let's follow after God's heart today to intercede for the people we know who do not know Jesus, snatching them from the fire in prayer.

Join us for prayer on Day 17 at:

www.acts413.net/deeperprayer
OR
www.strategicrenewal.com/21days-deeper-prayer

Day 18

Perfect Peace

Jim Maxim

You will keep in perfect peace all who trust in you, all whose thoughts are fixed on you!
—Isaiah 26:3 (NLT)

*When the servant of the man of God rose early in the morning and went out, behold, an army with horses and chariots was all around the city. And the servant [Gehazi] said, "Alas my master! What shall we do?" He said, "Do not be afraid, for those who are with us are more than those who are with them." Then Elisha prayed and said, "O LORD, please open his eyes that he may see." So **the LORD opened the eyes of the young man**, and he saw, and behold, the mountain was full of horses and chariots of fire all around Elisha.*
—2 Kings 6:15–17

The most interesting thing in this story is that nothing changed right away *except now the young man's eyes were opened.* The enemy was still surrounding Elisha and Gehazi, intent on their destruction. But now Gehazi could see what Elisha saw all along: God had sent horses and chariots of fire from heaven to make war on behalf of the prophet and his people. With God's help, Elisha was able to lead the army away from Israel and send them home.

Why was Elisha so calm in the face of danger? He trusted God and had *"perfect peace."*

Perfect means having all of the required or desirable elements, qualities, or characteristics to make something as good as it can possibly be. *Peace* means tranquility and freedom from disturbance.

> *You keep him in perfect peace whose mind is stayed on you, because he trusts in you.*   (Isaiah 26:3)

> *Those who love your instructions have great peace and do not stumble.*   (Psalm 119:165 NLT)

Is this something you believe can really be true? *Perfect peace?* In the nearly fifty years I have walked with God, I can assure you that this is very real and it's yours to have. I can also assure you it is found in only one place and that, my friend, is in His presence in your *"secret place,"* as Jesus called it.

> *Pray to your Father who is in the **secret place**; and your Father who sees in secret will reward you openly.*   (Matthew 6:6 NKJV)

God does not make this hard for us to experience, but we sometimes do. God continually goes out of His way by knocking on the door of our hearts and inviting us to come to Him. Remember the very first thing He did when Jesus died on the cross? He split the temple veil immediately so that we could have access to Him. (See Matthew 27:50–51.) God is holy and His attributes are perfect; in His presence, perfect peace exists because that's where our eyes are opened.

> *God is holy and His attributes are perfect;*
> *in His presence, perfect peace exists because that's where*
> *our eyes are opened.*

Our situations may not change immediately, but *we* can change because now we *see* with eyes of faith, and His presence brings perfect peace. Even if the enemy has us surrounded and in the natural, there is no possible way this can end well for us, God and one person is always a majority! Just ask Him to open your eyes and allow you to see Him and what His power is capable of and perfect peace will flood every aspect of your entire being. That's His promise, that's His Word, and that's for you, His child.

> **I pray that the eyes of your heart may be enlightened** in order *that you may know the hope to which he has called you, the riches of his glorious inheritance in his holy people, and his incomparably great power for us who believe.*   (Ephesians 1:18–19 NIV)

The apostle Paul wrote these words while he was in prison, so for him, this was a natural outpouring of his state of mind. Paul had experienced the supernatural; he knew it was truth, even behind prison walls, *and that's why his prayer is for our eyes to be opened!* Perfect peace can only come through the eyes of our understanding being enlightened as we enter behind the veil in prayer with humility and reverence for almighty God.

I've had many setbacks both personally and professionally as I'm sure you have. I've felt at times as if I was in a prison to the circumstances that confronted me, not seeing in the natural how it could possibly work out for my good. As I look back over those very rough times in my life, one thing always remained true: if I looked first at myself and took responsibility—spiritually, physically, mentally, and financially—and sought God in prayer with an honest heart, I was able to walk through whatever He allowed to come my way.

Spiritually

In the morning, start every conversation with God with humility and honesty about anything in life that may not be pleasing to Him. He knows it anyway, but He wants you to acknowledge it because sin is a snare that will entangle you. Honor God in your heart; He really is your heavenly Father, your Abba, your Dad.

> *You have not received a spirit that makes you fearful slaves. Instead, you received God's Spirit when he adopted you as his own children. Now we call him, "Abba, Father."*
>
> (Romans 8:15 NLT)

Physically

Your responsibility is to eat right, exercise regularly, get enough sleep, and take care of your body.

> *Don't you realize that your body is the temple of the Holy Spirit, who lives in you and was given to you by God?*
>
> (1 Corinthians 6:19 NLT)

Mentally

Learn as much as possible about the circumstances you are dealing with and get as much trusted professional advice as possible. Make any adjustments necessary. Pull down the negative thoughts that are sure to come; this is part of your daily success. Your mind can be more fully equipped in God's presence than anywhere else in the universe.

Financially

Hopefully, your financial plan—whether a family or business budget—is prepared for the setbacks that usually come in any effort. But if you are like me, and most people I know, some things can never be anticipated. Remember, whatever you are facing financially is not a surprise to God. He knew about this moment before the foundation of the world, and He has the answer for your need today. He is more than able to help us with our financial needs.

> *Seek the Kingdom of God above all else, and live righteously, and he will give you everything you need.*
>
> (Matthew 6:33 NLT)

I don't want to make light of what you are facing today. I have had moments of despair and unbelief. I've questioned my own ability, my faith, and my entire belief system. My wife would find me sitting awake at 3 a.m. wondering how I was going to be able to finish what we started. Building a business, I have been in trouble financially many different times; sometimes, everything felt completely overwhelming. But God was faithful and in the end, there was victory.

Where do you think I learned about God's ability? Where do you think any child of God grows the most? In the valley or on the mountaintop? God knows you're hurting and yet He will use this to bless you and build you into the person you really want to become for His glory.

> *Dear brothers and sisters, when troubles of any kind come your way, consider it an opportunity for great joy. For you know that when your faith is tested, your endurance has a chance to grow. So let it grow, for when your endurance is fully developed, you will be perfect and complete, needing nothing.*   (James 1:2–4 NLT)

That was not the answer I wanted to hear most of the time, but after I surrendered to Him, it made the most sense to me...and it brought me the greatest peace I have ever known.

God can do anything, and today we are going to pray and confess this out loud against the supernatural forces that are designed to fight against us. Today, we are going to pray, as Elisha did, and ask God to open our spiritual eyes so we can see things as they truly are, knowing *"there are more on our side than on theirs"* (2 Kings 6:16 NLT). Let's seek His beautiful face for His perfect peace, and then we will seek His all-powerful hand for the provision you need.

Join us for prayer on Day 18 at:

www.acts413.net/deeperprayer
OR
www.strategicrenewal.com/21days-deeper-prayer

Are You Really Praying in Jesus's Name?[14]

Daniel Henderson

*Whatever you ask in my name, this I will do, that the Father
may be glorified in the Son.*
—John 14:13

To pray in the Name of Christ…is to pray as one who is at
one with Christ, whose mind is the mind of Christ, whose
desires are the desires of Christ, and whose purpose is one
with that of Christ.
—Samuel Chadwick

In recent years, I have consistently begun my prayers with these
words: "Father God, in Jesus's name, and by the Holy Spirit…" This
affirmation actually changes the way I pray from the outset. In this day's
devotional, I want to propose that "in Jesus's name" was never designed
to be a tack-on at the end of our superficial requests. Rather, praying in
His name brings us into a reality that changes why, how, and what we
pray, from the very opening moment of our communion with God.

---

14. This chapter is adapted from Daniel Henderson's book *Transforming Prayer.*

TRUTH OR TRADITION?

Many believers seem to invoke *Jesus's name* in order to secure a prime parking place at the mall, a pay raise at work, or even the winning lottery ticket. Like me, maybe you have used "in Jesus's name" as a prayer-concluding formula to persuade God to give you something you really wanted, or thought you needed.

Most of us know that the idea of praying in Jesus's name is far beyond the routine of adding these three words on the end of our supplications. Yet, it is the traditional thing to do. In group or public prayers, it is a given that whoever prays better wrap it up with "in Jesus's name." When they fail to do so, they may get a few raised eyebrows and expressions of doubt about the spiritual legitimacy of their prayers. After all, will God really hear their prayers if they fail to include this three-word add-on?

JESUS'S NAME IN WORSHIP-BASED PRAYER

One of the amazing benefits of a worship-based, gospel-focused approach to prayer is that it fundamentally takes our eyes off ourselves and fixes them on Christ. We establish our prayer experience on Him, not ourselves. We seek to pray His thoughts, not our own. As the Spirit takes the conductor's wand of the Scriptures and orchestrates our praying, we cannot help but turn our eyes upon Jesus, as the beautiful old hymn encourages us:

> Turn your eyes upon Jesus,
> Look full in His wonderful face,
> And the things of earth will grow strangely dim,
> In the light of His glory and grace.[15]

---

15. Helen Howarth Lemmel, "The Heavenly Vision (Turn Your Eyes Upon Jesus)," 1922, public domain.

At that moment of wonder and intimacy, we are really in the place to truly pray in Jesus's name, regardless of the final three words of the prayer.

ASKING IN JESUS'S NAME

We all like guarantees. Advertisers tout "satisfaction guaranteed" and money-back guarantees on the products they want us to buy. Jesus, by the authority that only the Son of God can offer, makes a bold guarantee about prayer: *"Whatever you ask in my name, this I will do, that the Father may be glorified in the Son"* (John 14:13).

Jesus keeps speaking of the power of His name in prayer in this upper room interaction. In John 15:16, Christ expands our understanding of the necessity and proper use of His name: *"You did not choose me, but I chose you and appointed you that you should go and bear fruit and that your fruit should abide, so that whatever you ask the Father in my name, he may give it to you."* In John 16:23–24, He states, *"Truly, truly, I say to you, whatever you ask of the Father in my name, he will give it to you. Until now you have asked nothing in my name. Ask, and you will receive, that your joy may be full."*

In these verses, we are confronted with a condition and a result for all of our requests. The condition is that we ask in Jesus's name. Samuel Chadwick explained:

> Prayers offered in the Name of Christ are scrutinized and sanctified by His nature, His purpose, and His will. Prayer is endorsed by the Name when it is in harmony with the character, mind, desire, and purpose of the Name.[16]

---

16. Samuel Chadwick, *The Path of Prayer* (London: Hodder & Stoughton, 1936), 52.

In his excellent book *The God Who Hears*, W. Bingham Hunter summarizes the New Testament teaching about praying *in Jesus's name* with these four truths:

+ It seeks the glory of God.

+ Its foundation is the death, resurrection, and intercession of Jesus.

+ It is offered by Jesus's obedient disciples. Hunter points out that praying in Jesus's name is virtually synonymous with obedience to Jesus.

+ It asks what Jesus Himself would pray for.[17]

Hunter goes on to summarize:

> The shortest and perhaps the best answer is simply: *Jesus prayed according to the will of God*. And that, ultimately, is what it means for you and me to pray in Jesus's name—to pray according to the will of God.[18]

This explains why Jesus was so emphatic that *whatever* we ask in *His name*, we will receive.

Dr. Randal Roberts of Western Seminary in Portland, Oregon, says:

> It is to pray in a manner consistent with His values and purposes.... It is to pray with the glorification of God as the supreme motive; it is to pray as Jesus would pray were He in our circumstances; it is to pray as His followers who have been appointed as instruments of fruit-bearing in the outworking of His mission.... It is learning to ask for the good

---

17. W. Bingham Hunter, *The God Who Hears* (Downers Grove, IL: InterVarsity Press, 1986), 198.
18. Ibid.

things that He delights to give from the devoted heart that He delights to bless.[19]

EXPECT RESULTS!

What happens when we pray in Jesus's name? What is the ultimate purpose and result? According to Jesus's multiple commands in His upper room discourse, the outcomes of praying in His name are:

+ The Father will be glorified in the Son.

+ We bear fruit that remains.

+ Our joy will be full.

How many times have you been frustrated rather than fulfilled in prayer? Frustration comes from bombarding heaven with our self-styled ideas of what God should do to accomplish *our* will in heaven. Fulfillment comes from knowing that *His* will is being implemented on earth. Deep reward is found in knowing that the Father is glorified by our prayers, and that our relationship with Him is producing the lasting fruit of deep character and spiritual impact. Joy comes from this deep fulfillment.

So as we pray together, let's give it a thoughtful try: "Father God, in Jesus's name, and by the Holy Spirit…" And in all your praying in the days to come may we affirm a primary passion for the person and purposes of Jesus. It will change the way you commune with God and will transform your life.

Join us for prayer on Day 19 at:

www.acts413.net/deeperprayer
OR
www.strategicrenewal.com/21days-deeper-prayer

---

19. Randal Roberts, "Praying in the Name of Jesus," from *Giving Ourselves to Prayer—An Acts 6:4 Primer for Ministry* (Terre Haute, IN: PrayerShop Publishing, 2008), 47.

There Was a Believer

Jim Maxim

Now there was a believer in Damascus named Ananias. The Lord
spoke to him in a vision, calling, "Ananias!" "Yes, Lord!" he replied.
The Lord said, "Go over to Straight Street, to the house of Judas.
When you get there, ask for a man from Tarsus named Saul. He is
praying to me right now. I have shown him a vision of a man named
Ananias coming in and laying hands on him so he can see again.
—Acts 9:10–12 (NLT)

Two totally different men: one a committed believer in Jesus Christ, the other praying and seeking Him. A believer—and a praying man! That's all the first man was: a simple believer, nobody special, an everyday guy who had something different in his soul. *He was a believer*!

Let's look at this verse in Acts 9:10. Here is this average everyday believer named Ananias; we only hear about him this one time in the entire Bible. Yet, he was the guy God used to launch the greatest ministry in all the world next to Jesus Christ Himself! This man Ananias was directed to lay hands on Saul of Tarsus…who went on to write two thirds of the New Testament, testify to the most powerful leaders in the world, encourage the body of Christ for thousands of years, and revolutionize our understanding of God Himself!

I can't always put into words what I believe it means to simply *be a believer.* In our prayer time together today, you will hear my heart and my passion about this much clearer than in these words. I don't know about you, but so often, I'm tempted to feel like I'm *less than* most pastors and preachers. Hundreds of thousands of times, Satan has told me that I'm a loser and that I will never amount to anything, so I should just accept that and quit trying. The one thing in my life that I can point to as *the main source* of my success in anything I have ever done is *my prayer life.*

Prayer is the most powerful force ever known to mankind. The spiritual world knows this and that's why prayer is so very hard to maintain. But when we know this prayer struggle, we can submit it to God and through His Holy Spirit, our prayer time will become the most desired time in our day.

> *Ananias, an everyday believer who had a deep love for God, was used by God to launch the apostle Paul into his destiny for the Almighty and His church!*

Ananias, an everyday believer who had a deep love for God, was used by God to launch the apostle Paul into his destiny for the Almighty and His church! I want to be like that, don't you? I want to be so in tune with God that He flows through me daily to share His love and power with someone, somewhere, every single day. When you have a consistent prayer life, this automatically happens. How else could Ananias hear God's voice in this vision so clearly? If he wasn't in tune with God, he may have just rolled over and gone back to sleep.

Today is your day to stop rolling over! That's why we have embarked on this *21 Days of Deeper Prayer* with God; we want to hear His voice more clearly. Okay, so maybe we won't launch a man into a ministry like Paul's. But if we start praying every day with true faith, and waiting upon almighty God, calling out to Him, and standing in the gap for our pastor, his family, and the church staff, don't you think that the same God who blessed Paul will bless all of our church leaders and all of their families? Maybe what we are missing in the church at large are more people like Ananias, not more preachers.

God simply said that Ananias was *a believer*, just like you and me. Come on now and get excited with me—*we are believers!* I know that this is one of the areas of the church we just don't understand. God has pastors to bless, teach, and strengthen the church, *but the church is you and me.* We are *believers*, and we have God's calling and His anointing to *be* the church and do the works of Jesus. Let's agree today that this is the last time we are going to accept a second-place mentality that just because we don't have the title of pastor, preacher, or whatever, we aren't called to greater works for the kingdom of God. We do have the title of *Believer.*

Now let's go to almighty God together and confess our sin of unbelief and perhaps laziness for not acting like a true believer. Our pastors, their families, and the world around us need the power of God within us to bless them and help them to become what God has destined for them to be.

Today we will pray the Scriptures over our loved ones and all of the burdens you may have in your life. We are going to go before almighty God and believe Him and His promises to us and pray them out loud together. We are going to ask God to help us to never limit Him in our lives and open up our minds to see Him as He actually is, the Supreme Ruler of the Universe. There is *nothing* He cannot do.

Join us for prayer on Day 20 at:

www.acts413.net/deeperprayer
OR
www.strategicrenewal.com/21days-deeper-prayer

Day 21

Moving the Hand that Moves
the World

Jim Maxim

Prayer moves the hand that moves the world.
—*Charles C. Spurgeon*

Then the LORD relented and did not bring on his people the
disaster he had threatened.
—Exodus 32:14 (NIV)

If that nation, concerning which I have spoken, turns from its evil,
I will relent of the disaster that I intended to do to it.
—Jeremiah 18:8

We have come to the end of our *21 Days of Deeper Prayer* together.
What I want to do on this last day is to pour my heart out before you.
The need for prayer and the power of prayer in our lives is the greatest
thing God has done for us, made possible through the sacrifice of Jesus
Christ. The Lord listens to our fervent prayers and even changes His

mind in response to them. The very idea that we have the privilege to know the Creator of all mankind and interact with Him whenever we want, and then *not do it*…I can't find the words to describe it other than prideful stupidity.

Here are just a few of God's attributes: the infinity of God, the eternity of God, the holiness of God, the oneness of God, the impeccability of God, the transcendence of God, the eminence of God, the omnipresence of God, the mutability of God, the omnipotence of God, the supremacy of God, the sovereignty of God, the veracity of God, the mystery of God, the goodness of God, the kindness of God, the grace of God, the mercy of God, the love of God, the faithfulness of God, the justice of God, the joy of God, the peace of God…

Knowing that we can have access to all that God is and has, and then to dismiss it, stupidity doesn't even begin to describe the misappropriation of these attributes. The Bible tells us, *"Pride goes before destruction, and a haughty spirit before a fall"* (Proverbs 16:18).

The idea that I could speak face to face with my God and not do it is simply a sin. The greatest thing in my life, the greatest thing that I can ever do, and the greatest thing that I will *ever* do is bow before almighty God, worship Him, honor Him, and declare His sovereignty, His authority, and His power over my life and the lives of all of my family.

I love God; I need God; I want God; I must have God. My mornings are crying out to Him. My mornings start with being in God's presence. I need the very presence of God to touch me every single day. I want my Father to minister to me. I want my Father to touch me, encourage me, and allow me to sense His presence. I want almighty God to fellowship with me. I want the Father, Jesus, and the Holy Spirit to be in my life in such a way that everywhere I go, men and women will see the very presence of God in my life. I pray in the name of Jesus Christ that

God Almighty would permit me to have the ability to describe Him to others.

The greatest thing that I ask of God is the ability to describe Him to somebody else. The greatest thing that I'll ever do is to lead a sinner to the cross of Jesus Christ. The most important part of my life is to seek someone who doesn't know God, doesn't know His attributes, and doesn't know how much He longs to be with them and how much He longs to have fellowship with them, and to describe the love of Jesus Christ on the cross for them. The idea that the Holy Spirit of almighty God can take up residence in me, flow through me, and use me to bring others to the cross of Jesus Christ is the greatest truth that I will ever comprehend.

I *must* have God's presence in my life! I will pursue almighty God more than anything else in my life because I know that I need Him. I cannot serve God without His anointing, without His strength, without His presence, or without Him enabling me to serve Him. And yet I know that God longs to be with me.

Why does God long to be with me? I'll never truly understand other than to say that it's because of His Holiness and His love, His attributes, His kindness, His goodness, His grace, and His love towards mankind. Those are the only reasons I can begin to understand why God would want to be with me.

Yes, I need God so much in my life, and I long for *you* to understand just how much God wants to be with you. God is longing for His church, His bride, to come and be with Him, to fellowship with Him, and to desire to be with Him. God has so much for His church, but His church is just not entering into receiving what He has for them.

"Thus the LORD *used to speak to Moses face to face, as a man speaks to his friend"* (Exodus 33:11). Let's ask God to allow us to be His friend

as Moses was. This is what He wants us to ask Him. God wants to draw us into His presence. God is longing for us to ask Him to let us be His friends.

When we get to heaven, we will see God face to face; we will see His holiness and understand His divinity. Why not go to Him right now, today, and ask Him to allow you to understand Him more and truly be His friend...*on earth as it is in heaven.*

On this final day of our prayer journey, join us in prayer to our Father who loves us at:

www.acts413.net/deeperprayer
OR
www.strategicrenewal.com/21days-deeper-prayer

About the Authors

Nearly forty years ago, Jim Maxim was at the lowest point of his life. As he lay at death's door, Jim's mother prayed for his soul. God answered her prayer and Jim's life was claimed, redeemed, and transformed for Jesus Christ. The dramatic story of Jim's conversion is found in his book *Face-to-Face with God*.

Jim served in the U.S. Marine Corps and created multiple successful companies in the automotive industry. He also served God in prison ministries, as a speaker, and as a board member of ministries like Hope Pregnancy Center and the Valley Forge Leadership Prayer Breakfast.

In 2011, Jim and his wife, Cathy, founded Acts413 Ministries, where they evangelize, counsel, and minister in the name of Jesus all over the world. Jim prays and leads others in intercessory prayer for pastors, their families, and churches.

The highlight of Acts413 Ministries is city-wide prayer gatherings held throughout the United States. They serve as a catalyst to mobilize the body of Christ to intercede for our pastors and their families. Christians from every denomination, socioeconomic background, culture, and color worship and pray through Scripture in the name of Jesus Christ. While the prayers may cover many topics, there is always a special focus on interceding for pastors, their families, and churches. Jim firmly believes that the church is the primary plan for ministering to God's people on earth.

The Maxims have three sons, three daughters-in-law, and three grandchildren.

As a senior pastor for over two decades, Daniel Henderson brought prayer-based revitalization to numerous churches. Now, as the president of Strategic Renewal, he is dedicating his full-time efforts to help congregations across the country and world experience renewal.

Daniel is sought after for his expertise in leading corporate prayer. He has authored numerous books on biblical leadership and prayer, including *Old Paths, New Power* and *Transforming Prayer: How Everything Changes When You Seek God's Face*.